Until Further Notice

Until Further Notice

A Year in Pandemic Time

AMY KALER

UNIVERSITY *of* **ALBERTA** PRESS

Published by

University of Alberta Press
1-16 Rutherford Library South
11204 89 Avenue NW
Edmonton, Alberta, Canada T6G 2J4
amiskwaciwâskahikan | Treaty 6 | Métis Territory
uap.ualberta.ca | uapress@ualberta.ca

Library and Archives Canada Cataloguing in Publication

Title: Until further notice : a year in pandemic time / Amy Kaler.
Names: Kaler, Amy, author.
Description: Includes bibliographical references.
Identifiers: Canadiana (print) 2022025026X | Canadiana (ebook) 2022025530X | ISBN
    9781772126259 (softcover) | ISBN 9781772126600 (EPUB) | ISBN 9781772126617 (PDF)
Subjects: LCSH: Kaler, Amy. | LCSH: COVID-19 Pandemic, 2020- | LCGFT: Autobiographies.
    | LCGFT: Creative nonfiction.
Classification: LCC PS8621.A466 U58 2022 | DDC C818/.603—dc23

First edition, first printing, 2022.
First printed and bound in Canada by Houghton Boston Printers, Saskatoon, Saskatchewan.
Copyediting and proofreading by Maya Fowler Sutherland.

University of Alberta Press is committed to protecting our natural environment. As part of our efforts, this book is printed on Enviro Paper: it contains 100% post-consumer recycled fibres and is acid- and chlorine-free.

University of Alberta Press gratefully acknowledges the support received for its publishing program from the Government of Canada, the Canada Council for the Arts, and the Government of Alberta through the Alberta Media Fund.

Unless we become aware of the transitions that are occurring all the time within us, unless we learn to let experience play upon our inner lives as on a finely tuned instrument, we will try to manufacture inner intensity from the outside, we will bang our very bones to roust our souls. We crave radical ruptures when we have allowed the nerves of our inner lives to go numb. But after these ruptures—the excitement or the tragedy, the pleasure or the pain—the mind returns to what it was, the soul quicksilvers off from the pierce of experience, and the kingdom of boredom, which could be the kingdom of God, begins the clock-tick towards its next collapse.

—Christian Wiman, *My Bright Abyss*

If you see something, say something.

—Slogan seen in airports, warning travellers to be alert for signs of danger

Contents

Spring 2020

Summer 2020

Fall 2020

Winter 2021

Spring 2021

Coda

Acknowledgements

I'm grateful to Rosie Kaler-Thompson for her resilience and spirit.

I also want to acknowledge the people that made up my in-person social world in Edmonton during the pandemic: especially Michel Figeat, but also Sara Dorow, Cressida Heyes, Jonathan Leggo, Debra Davidson, Rhonda Breitkreuz, Michele Harvey, and Heather Young-Leslie. The people I connected with by screen and phone also meant a great deal to me: especially Jennifer Beeman, but also Martha Easton, Leela MadhavaRau, Heidi Ragsdale, Liz Derbecker, Elizabeth Turner, Rachel Barney, Leslie Beckmann, Beatrice Upenieks, Raina Feldman Wells, Nigel Crawhall, Michael Kaler, Hilary Kaler, Wendy Banks, John Faithful Hamer, and Nadia Tomy.

I remember my father, John Otis Kaler, 1932–2020. I don't know if he would have liked this book, but I wish he could have read it.

This book was written in Edmonton / amiskwaciwâskahikan on Treaty 6 territory, a traditional meeting ground, gathering place, and travelling route to the Cree, Saulteaux, Blackfoot, Métis, Dene and Nakoda Sioux.

Acknowledgements

Introduction

When the pandemic began, I decided I was going to write about it. I didn't know what this writing was going to look like, because although I have written books before, I have never set myself a project like this, which begins by telling myself, "You are living through a historically significant experience about which you have no choice. You must only try to be a faithful witness to that experience."

This impulse to write grew out of the condition that Sianne Ngai calls "stuplimity": the mix of shock and overwhelm with boredom and aimlessness that closes off access to full expression of the grand emotions, like sorrow or anger, and leaves you marooned in the shallow waters of irritation, fretfulness, and anxiety. You can drown in shallow water just as completely as you can drown in a raging ocean storm, and the book you're holding, or rather my idea of this book, is one of the floating things I grabbed onto so as not to drown.

Ngai was writing about visual and literary arts when she came up with the idea of the stuplime, exemplified by slapstick comedy in which banana peels endlessly exhaust the capacity of comedians to fall down and get up again, or art installations consisting of laser printers that spew out variations on insincere apologies hour after hour. Ngai cites Samuel Beckett as the secular high priest of stuplimity, with his dimwitted characters buried up to the neck in stuff that impedes their movement, muttering pointlessly and incoherently while nothing happens. The Covid pandemic gave me stuplimity overload in my daily life.

The tedium of stuplimity is related to its aimlessness and inaction in the face of something enormous. Stuplime affect is the suspension of the possibility of catharsis, the impossibility of working out or working through the enormous thing that has you in its grip. It doesn't translate easily into the kind of purposive action, either personal or political, that I had relied on in previous experiences of low affect or mood.

Stuplimity is depressing, but it isn't depression. It was new to me, and for that reason at least mildly interesting, and so I wanted to write about it, even if I couldn't actually do much about it.

I knew what I didn't want to write. Perhaps in reaction against my training as a social scientist, I did not want to produce a work of social analysis. I did not want to stand back and situate Covid as a case of some broader phenomenon, or to name and detail the structural forces that brought the world to where it is today, shut down and careening and possibly doomed. I know other people will do that much better than I can. I also didn't want to write a sort of dear-diary account of my life during the pandemic day by day. I needed chronology to structure my thoughts (and indeed, time and its measurement would become a major theme in these thoughts), but I didn't want the particulars of my life to be the reason this book exists.

What I wanted to do was to produce an account, or a series of short accounts, of how the pandemic was afflicting my thought processes and my experiences of being-in-the-world, with an emphasis on cognitive warps and distortions. This inevitably meant that I was noting down a lot of small Covid stories—this happened to me, or to someone I know, on this day, at this place. Here is what I did or saw or heard, and here is where it led me. Here's a motorcycle accident, here's a memory of a TV show, here's a dream, here are things I found in the back of a cabinet, here's an article about the North Pole, here's an odd sensation, which is not exactly embodied but also not exactly not. By putting these stories together, even if they don't fall into a smooth and logical sequence of ideas, I might be able to create some meaning out of this pandemic.

I do so in the spirit of the one choice that I have about this pandemic—I can either live through it and be miserable, or I can live through it and be miserable and learn something. (This choice has presented itself to me at other moments in my life—divorce, the death of a parent, significant illness. I can't control what happens, but I can watch and listen and move towards understanding.)

As far as I know I have been Covid-negative all year. I have not been infected with the virus, but I know myself as being bent by it, like a tree slowly tipping and twisting, pulled off its course by months or years of relentless hurricane wind. I wanted to be as observant and analytical as possible, in the hope that one thing, possibly the only honest thing, I could do with a slowly warping mind is to use it to note the contouring and graining of its own warping.

What follows is fragmented and not always linear. I begin on March 14, 2020, just before the day that my city shut down, and I end exactly a year later, on March 14, 2021, with vaccines rolling out across Canada, although not yet to me. This is an account of only the first year of the pandemic; I am under no illusion that it is over.

I wrote these entries in real time, not in retrospect (with one exception: the entry titled "Leonard Cohen at the Whistle Stop Café" was written in early May 2021 but pertains to the events at that café that began earlier in January). In July 2020, when I was first writing about the disorienting effects of seeing into people's home on Zoom screens, I didn't know that I would still be on Zoom eight months later. In the late fall, when I wrote about the despair attending the second wave of Covid, I didn't know that numbers would fall off to a level that permitted a cautious and contested reopening in February 2021. And as I was trying to imagine the future in the summer, I didn't know about the vaccines that were even then in development and trials and would soon displace case counts as the centre of gravity for public talk about Covid.

Because I have a professional background in population health and the sociology of infectious disease, Covid infused my professional life. I was in no way a "frontline worker" who tried to help the sick and protect the healthy, but I got called a lot by radio and television journalists, locally and nationally, to provide some context for the pandemic in Alberta and offer informed opinion on how the provincial government was handling it. ("With all the foresight and wisdom of a drunken sailor" was usually my response.) To friends, I referred to this work as being the plague whisperer. Plague whispering doesn't feature in this account, partly because I know there will be epidemiological histories of Covid in Canada published in the next few years, and partly because the entries that make up this book are mostly things that happened to me when I wasn't in gear as an academic sociologist. Nonetheless, I do have some expert knowledge of the course of pandemics, and that knowledge leaches into the writing in some places (most notably in the entry titled "Personal Responsibility").

Now as I'm writing this in March 2021, I still don't know which facets of my life have been irrevocably changed by the pandemic, and what changes will prove to be transient or ephemeral. Of all the ways that the coronavirus has warped the pathways of my mind, I don't know which are durable in their crookedness and which are pliant, remoulding themselves to their old straightforward form once the pandemic has passed over. What I do know is that I am not the same person as the one whose return from Ottawa in March opens these accounts.

The Beginning

This is how Covid began to change my mind.

In mid-March, I was at a four-day meeting in Ottawa, ending on the 14th. I spent most of those days in a meeting room with academics from across Canada and a few from Europe. I had heard about the coronavirus by that time, of course, but assumed it was something like H1N1 or SARS, at worst—a serious event, a reminder of how interconnected the world was and how swift contagion could be, but ultimately, not something that would really change my life. If I thought about it at all, it was to wonder vaguely why it was still on the news, why it hadn't gone away yet. Throughout February, I had been party to discussions about cancelling these Ottawa meetings; I listened and nodded soberly, but privately I thought this was a bit alarmist. It was going to go away.

Except it didn't. And over a few days in March, it got much worse.

Throughout the course of the meeting, news of the virus seeped into the conference rooms, getting worse and worse. Furtive checking of phones during sessions increased. At coffee breaks, we traded bits of what we had heard, over snacks that moved from communal fruit plates to individually-wrapped pastries with tongs. In hindsight, these were the first signs of social distancing. The man sitting next to me muttered that if the schools were going to be closed in Ontario he was going to pack up his kids and send them off to his mother in St. Vincent, where she could keep them occupied in their rural home-place, rather than in germy Toronto.

The anxiety humming under the business of the meeting reminded me of the evening of the 2016 American elections. I spent that evening in the audience of a youth sporting event, giving no more than half my attention to what was happening on the competition floor and the rest gradually accreting to my phone and the green-and-black text screen, lighting up with announcements that yet another state had fallen. I couldn't believe it was happening, but it was happening. The meeting in Ottawa, budgets and spreadsheets on the overhead projector juxtaposed with furtive checking of phones under desks, had the same quality of the mundane and the catastrophic jostling each other in my awareness.

I went up to my hotel room during one of the breaks and pressed the elevator button with my elbow, wondering whether at some future moment I would remember that action as the first time I altered my behaviour because of the virus. I tried not to think about the surface of the elevator button.

On the day I left Ottawa, I was booked on an evening flight, which meant I had almost a full day to myself. I like walking and I like Ottawa, so under normal circumstances this would have been a good thing. But this time, as I started to notice the first "closed" signs appearing on shops, and the first masked pedestrians, and the first conscious and careful maintenance of personal space in public thoroughfares, I became aware that impatience, yearning, and worry were building up inside me, pulling me like a compass towards the airport. I wanted to be there right away, even though it would be four or five or six hours before the flight left, and more than just getting to the airport, I wanted to get through security, past the document check, down the gangway, and onto the plane. I wanted to be absolutely certain that I was on my way back to Edmonton—back home—and that I would be there by nightfall.

In my mind, I saw images of crowds pushing to get the last seats on the last plane out of here (wherever "here" might be), and of airport destination boards lighting up with cancellations. I worried that it might actually be possible to close the borders of a province. I knew that my images and my worries did not make sense. I had confirmed and reconfirmed my reservation, there were no indications that anything was being cancelled, and even if I somehow did not get on that flight, the worst that could happen was that I would spend another few days in Ottawa. In the course of several decades travelling the world for work, I had had unexpected travel setbacks before but had always returned home in one piece. This, today, was only a matter of getting from Ottawa to Edmonton. But the fear that I wouldn't make it home in time (in time for what?) slowly grew.

I finally gave in to anxiety and got a taxi to the airport much sooner than I needed to. The taxi driver, from North Africa, had heard that people were starting to descend on Costco and bulk supermarkets, buying up tinned fish and toilet paper. He laughed about this, noting that in his home country anyone with means always put several weeks of food aside in case of unrest and disruption. It was only the poor or the improvident who had to panic-buy when rumours of crisis started gathering. According to him, if no one was hoarding bottled water, things weren't that bad yet.

At the airport, the Air Canada lounge was sour with anxiety, like everywhere else. Parliament had just been suspended, and my flight was the first one out of Ottawa to western Canada. Cranky and nervous members of parliament were on their way home, loading up on the free drinks in the lounge, and once in the air, badgering the flight attendant for more drinks and complaining about the selection of vodka. I saw my own member of parliament, the only New Democratic Party member from Alberta, working quietly on her laptop. We knew each other slightly, because I had volunteered for her campaign six months ago. I asked if she needed a ride home from the airport when we got to Edmonton. I felt that I should make some sort of gesture of solidarity, in acknowledgement of our strange circumstances, without knowing exactly why.

We got on the plane, it went up, and it came down in Edmonton four hours later. Towing my carry-on bag behind me, I walked through an almost-empty terminal towards the ground transportation exit. I wondered if everywhere was going to look like this from now on—shuttered, stilled, and inhabited only by people moving purposefully to their destination.

That word, "purposeful." It kept echoing in my mind over the next few days. I knew that in the social bubble that I inhabit, that of well-educated middle-class liberal-leaning CBC-listening, letter-to-the-editor-writing Canadians, I was going to hear a lot about making the most of the pandemic and what we could learn from it about our world and what it all means. Meaning, purpose! I have been socialized into looking for these things always. I'm a sociologist, it's what I do. But while I didn't want to just let the pandemic wash over me while I waited for it to go away, I also had a visceral aversion to contributing to the tide of "think pieces," political manifestos, and authoritative accounts of what the pandemic is teaching us about the world. There are many writers who are better at that than I am. I didn't, and still don't, know what the pandemic means for the world. I only know what it is like to be me in the middle of it.

The rest of this book is exactly that—what it's like to be me in the midst of a pandemic. I'm a middle-aged white woman of settler background, a single parent who lives in east-central Edmonton with a teenage daughter and a cat. I've got several good friends in the city and more in other parts of the world, where I bounced around for the first thirty-five years of my life before landing here. I have a long-term partner who lives out of town. My family of origin lives in central Canada, and over the course of the pandemic my parents, in their 80s, went into a steep health decline and my father passed away. I'm a professor at the University of Alberta, which means that I wasn't laid off and my income remained stable, and also that I switched to working entirely from home at the very outset of the pandemic. My orbit shrank down to my apartment and the North Saskatchewan River valley (about which much more later), with a few necessary outposts of groceries, library books and craft supplies forming a perimeter. I had to learn to do a lot of things differently once Covid hit.

In particular, I had to learn to love Edmonton during the pandemic. I'd lived here for twenty years in a spirit of tolerant adaptation. Edmonton is not Manhattan or Paris or London, and it's not even Toronto or Montreal or Vancouver. I'd become accustomed to thinking of *real* urban life as something that happened somewhere else, where the streets were not quite so wide and the suburbs weren't quite so new and there were buildings and public spaces that had been around for centuries. I knew people who loved Edmonton, but I assumed that love was either the unquestioning fondness for the place where you grew up, or was acquired later as part of the whole western prairie package involving junior-league hockey, dually pickups, five-bedroom suburban homes, and voting conservative. Edmonton was the place where I lived and it was fine as far as it went, but it wasn't the place where I belonged. I belonged somewhere more…interesting. Lively. Intellectual. More used bookstores and cafés. I was stationed up here at fifty-three degrees north first for the duration of my job and then for the duration of my daughter's childhood.

In short, I was an obnoxious elitist and that elitism got knocked out of me while I was tethered in Edmonton by the virus. I don't miss it at all. I found that not only did I have to grow into Edmonton in order to love it, I also had to really work for that love. Montreal and Toronto and Vancouver are easy sells when it comes to urban ambience. It's not hard to be a partisan of these places—Leonard Cohen and Margaret Atwood and Stanley Park and Queen West and St-Viateur Bagels. In order to love Edmonton, I first had to work at inhabiting Edmonton, which was a process as much corporeal as sentimental or intellec-tual. I had to walk trails, climb into valleys, get down to the river and scrabble along the spots where the banks were wearing thin. I also had to really look at my neighbourhood, instead of just passing through it. My neighbourhood may not be much, but it's now mine in a way that it wasn't before the pandemic.

Other things are now mine too, including things that aren't as happy as pushing my roots down into the soil of Edmonton. These things include a vexed relationship to the passage of time, a near-con-stant state of anxiety, and unwished-for deterioration in my ability to think clearly. These are why I say that the pandemic changed my mind, and they occupy much of the book ahead.

At the beginning, I did not know what the weeks and months ahead would bring. I knew that I was going into a long period of living in a city that was manifesting all the signs that in a person would signal depression: Withdrawal. Immobility. Avoidance of social contact. Circuits of anxious rumination, in the form of social media chat groups and channels devoted to the pandemic. Foreclosure of the future, as all plans for spring, and then summer, and then fall, and then winter are withdrawn. Eternal and inescapable present, as we didn't know when the future would resume. Anhedonia, loss of pleasure, as playgrounds and parks are cordoned off with yellow tape. Empty buses, empty streets, empty trains, empty stores, empty parking lots. Minds and hearts full.

Spring 2020

Before, After

As I'm doing the things I need to do in daily life, I'm conscious of a new intensity of experience, a heightened attention to how things have changed. The feel of the cloth mask on my face when I go to get cash at the bank and the silence of the university campus when I go in to pick up my books remind me that the world has changed. Every experience is double, or even triple: there's the way it was, the way it is now, and maybe the way it will be, when the pandemic fires have burned themselves out. Buying groceries, going to school, going for a walk, planning for retirement, finding elder care for my parents in Ontario, planning for teaching classes in the fall—I remember how it was, and I'm struggling with how it is, but I don't know how it will be.

The future is unknown, and the present is provisional, improvised. I'm figuring out ways to get around the pandemic—how do I do all those things that I need to do under these new conditions of places that are empty, institutions that are closed, people and resources that have disappeared? Also, how long is this going to last? I should probably be focusing on the right-now, because it's become a lot more complicated than it was a month ago, but I don't yet know how to think about these complications, how to put them into some sort of temporal flow.

Are they temporary aberrations, like the bus route to downtown being rerouted while construction's underway for the LRT, or is this bus heading off the map altogether, with the gridlines of the known cartography vanishing in the rearview mirror? The bus shelters along the street outside my building have now acquired yellow caution tape criss-crosses and laminated posters indicating that they are out of service "until further notice." Waiting for that notice, existing in this indeterminate and weird present—I've never done anything like this before, and it's going to be hard.

I wish I could say something more profound than "I think it's going to be hard," but I'm suffering a loss of words to describe how this feels. Language is being evacuated from me. It is strange to be having a life-defining experience that will split the world into before and after, and to know that I am having such an experience, and to know that everyone else in the world is having a similar experience at the same time. I find it almost impossible to think about anything else, yet I know I can't speak truthfully about it to anyone (if I were actually speaking to anyone, which I am not, because I'm staying locked down and socially distant). My words will always be too few and too late to convey the intensities of the pandemic.

I am very conscious of the pandemic as a world-altering event. I know the self who emerges at the end of it, if or when there is an end, will not be the self who is writing these words just after getting home from Ottawa. But as yet, I have no language for this transformation.

I think back to those corny time capsules we buried at elementary school in grade four marked with "Open In 2075." It took a conscious effort to believe that 2075 might really exist. Even the number on the calendar seemed wrong—in my nine-year-old experience, dates started with 19, not 20.

I used to picture the scene when the capsule was exhumed a hundred years later, a circle of spectators watching as it was lifted clear of the dirt in some alien future, maybe with sleek streamlined buildings and hovercars. However, I never wondered what it would be like inside the time capsule, whether you'd know from the inside that time was passing or be able to sense that you were approaching the hundred-year mark and the opening of the ground above you. My life feels like an enclosed time capsule now, underground in the endless moment before the shovels hit the dirt and the lid is lifted off.

Concentration

My concentration is shot. I can follow the staccato tempo of emails— short bursts, finished off with a firm click and send—but reading anything longer than a few hundred words produces a blitz of constant self-administered interruptions, like small electric shocks. Did I feed the cat, does the cat need to be fed, I should check whether someone has emailed me back, where's the laundry detergent, I should move the laundry, this book is hard to follow, I give up.

My psychic world is taking on the shape of the external world, news of which is delivered in a blinding stream of bulletins and updates, with rapid reverses, contradictions, and stops and starts of information. The schools are opening next week, the schools are closed until the end of the year. You shouldn't touch your mail without gloves, you can't pick up the virus from paper. Millions might die, but there's a new vaccine, but the new vaccine doesn't work. The US is sending troops to the border, Trump changed his mind.

The mental energy required to attend to these switchbacks and hairpin turns is sucked directly out of whatever reservoir supplies the power for mindful contemplation, or even for calm deliberation. That minor muscle twitch in the corner of my left eye, which I get when I haven't had enough sleep over a long period, is back, an irregular syncopation that's almost impossible to ignore.

I'm not the only person losing the ability to concentrate. I see a lot of jokes going around on social media about having lost time during the pandemic: needing reminders as to what day of the week it is (emails from my church begin with "TODAY IS TUESDAY"), not being sure whether the meal in front of you is lunch or dinner ("wait, did we eat this already?," my daughter asks). I'm feeling adrift in time too.

And I'm also experiencing a deficit in my sense of place—where exactly am I and why am I here? Two days ago, I went out for a rigorously constitutional walk in my neighbourhood. Within three blocks I had gotten completely lost as to which direction I was heading—am I walking towards downtown, which is north, or away from the river, which is south?

Then the next day I lost my car near Strathearn Community League. I usually have a sort of non-material imaginary filament attaching me to the car, which fails sometimes in crowded parking garages in which every floor looks the same, but is generally strong and taut when I'm out in the city. I have a feel for where I was when I parked. But today the tether failed. I could not orient myself by knowing where my Subaru was, and had to wander in purposeful yet random circles in a part of the city that I used to know well, until I stopped short, because there was the car right in front of me. This pleasant neighbourhood had taken on the character of an anonymous parking garage. Every spot has become like every other spot, and none of them are welcoming or memorable.

Returns

During the pandemic, I'm revisiting dispositions from earlier times in my life. By dispositions, I mean the nexus (nexuses?) of particular desires/aversions, of opportunities for action, and of decisions that need to be made. Everything new is a return to some older way of being. The pandemic is historically unique, yet I keep experiencing déjà vu.

Seeing empty shelves in a shop reawakens the time that I lived in Zimbabwe in the 1990s, when the Zimbabwean currency was non-convertible and inflation was starting to go crazy, with the result that imported or manufactured goods started disappearing. I remember the growing tally of items that "went short": salt, sugar, cooking oil, soap. Now it's toilet paper, yeast, and cleaning products. People are starting to line up outside Costco and Safeway to get these goods, and the sight of the queues produces a strange mental overlay of Harare circa 1991. The clothes, cityscape, and skin colour of the people in the queue are all different, but the mild ennui of waiting outside a shop for my turn to step into the role of consumer is the same. I even feel a frisson of competence, thinking, "yeah, been there and done that, lining up for basic goods, here I go again."

Weekend mornings with my daughter reawaken earlier parenting moments and the contrast between the warm inertia of inside-the-house and the bracing but slightly intimidating opportunities of outside-the-house. When she's in her room for hours listening to music on the weekend, I'm predisposed to chivvying her out. You can't stay in your room all weekend, there's a whole world out there, what are your plans, let's go! Do you want to turn into one of those urban hermits, like the Japanese *hikikomori* who never leave their rooms? (And more selfishly, do I want to be the mother who let her kid turn into a *hikikomori*?). Then I remember: that disposition does not fit anymore. Staying inside, in your room, watching Netflix and listening to Spotify playlists is no longer just the path of least resistance, something that parents let their kids do when the parents are too busy or lazy to do their jobs properly. Withdrawal from the outside world has a new meaning when there's a virus out there. Seclusion and reserve are the new right thing.

(I had to google "hikikomori" to be sure I was spelling it right. In my family sociology classes, I've taught about the sociological and psychological correlates of this tendency among highly stressed young men in Japan and South Korea to withdraw into their bedrooms and never emerge, so I had some passing familiarity with the phenomenon. In the year of the pandemic, however, googling brings up a crop of very recent articles about what *hikikomori* can teach the rest of us about living in seclusion. They've been doing it for years in their bedrooms reorganized into living capsules, with multiple video screens, stacks of books and magazines and clothes hung neatly from rods. The *hikikomori* is reconfigured as a sage, an expert in the dispositions of quarantine).

I meet my dispositions when I'm outdoors as well as inside. Walking along the upper path in the Mill Creek Ravine, I notice a group of children playing on a plateau just below me, between me and the water. They've rigged up a sort of slide that shoots them down from the level of the path into the middle of a small grove of aspen and poplar, where the other kids are whooping and cheering each slider. I smiled benignly and thought, "the Upper P in the evening. Lovely."

But the Upper P was long ago and far away: it was the upper playing field of the camp in Ontario where I spent many summers, first as camper and then as staff. It too was a grassy meadow surrounded by small trees, but it's long gone now, parcelled out for time-share vacation rentals. The kids in the ravine aren't me and my friends as campers, they're local kids who are playing in the clearing because the playgrounds have been cordoned off with yellow caution tape, a sight I'm coming to find almost unbearably poignant. My memory is enveloping the kids in the meadow with a sort of golden nostalgic glow, transporting their pandemic entertainments into my own history.

Breathe

George Floyd is dead in Minneapolis. He was murdered by a police officer who compressed his throat by kneeling on him, for eight minutes, in front of a crowd, while being filmed by a young woman on her phone. Floyd's last known words were "I can't breathe," over and over again. The crowd became increasingly agitated by the slow killing, and bystanders can be heard on the recording calling 911, fruitlessly calling the cops on the cops. Minneapolis was burning for three days after Floyd's murder, and because I went to graduate school in Minneapolis and lived in a neighbourbood adjacent to the one in which Floyd was killed, I can visualize the blocks, the streets, the stores that burned down.

I'm watching all this from Canada, across a border sealed by the pandemic, and I'm horrified. It's not happening in another country, it's happening in my own. I'm a dual citizen, half-American, and the shock and outrage are mixed with a kind of desperate sadness. Those are my people—the ones marching in the streets but also the ones killing unarmed Black men and terrorizing communities of colour. I want more than anything to disavow them, but I can't. And I can't do anything to expiate my share of this American sin other than a few Venmo transfers to the Southern Poverty Law Center.

In the four years since Trump was elected, I've lost any vestiges of surprise that such things could happen in this country, but the shock is still there. It *should* not happen like this, it *must not* happen like this. I've lived outside the US for more years than I've lived in it, but the myth of American exceptionalism, American decency and fairness, still has a hold on me. I think of what Carl Oglesby, one of the radical founders of Students for a Democratic Society in 1965, said about the country that "mouthed my liberal values and broke my American heart." This foundational wound of the United States is open again, the blood flowing on the screens I can't stop watching, and the pandemic compounds my heartbreak.

The Covid pandemic, like the killing of Black men by police, is an extinction that didn't have to happen. It could have been stopped. But the people in power (who, especially since Trump was elected, are overwhelmingly white) decided not to stop it.

I'm thinking of George Floyd, who couldn't breathe, and all the people who've died from hypoxia subsequent to Covid, who also couldn't breathe, even with oxygen cannulas and non-rebreather masks and mechanical ventilation. I know from epidemiological reports that the people asphyxiating in hospital wards or homes are disproportionately Black or Asian, or Native American. So little air. There is not enough oxygen to keep us all alive.

Airport Security

Everything is like airport security now. At the time I came back from Ottawa, I didn't realize how much of my outside-the-home life would come to resemble post-9/11 getting-on-a-plane. At Save-On, lineups are organized by ropes, and uniformed personnel sorting visitors through entry stations, and instead of screening machines and conveyor belts, pump stations of sanitizer, which every shopper must apply. Does this make us safer? Do the lines and the ropes exert a soothing influence, with their appearance of order? Or do they just remind us that we are not in fact safe?

The only reason for a security line in an airport is the possibility that one of the other travellers, scratching their head or unzipping their carry-on, might have a bomb. Where are the bombs here, outside Save-On, and which of my fellow shoppers has one? Edmonton has become a departure gate, and I don't know when the flight is leaving or where we will arrive when the flight is over.

Crossing New Thresholds

The lines between private and public spaces, or between domestic spaces and everything else, are vanishing. What is private is now public, in a strange way. Even as the shared spaces of the city, where I used to hurry past other people, are emptying out (I could walk down the middle of Whyte Avenue with my eyes closed and not worry about traffic). I am being drawn into the home-places of friends, acquaintances, and complete strangers.

It's a technology thing. In the course of my work as a university professor, I'm seeing living rooms and bedrooms and jury-rigged office spaces on Zoom and Skype, and if I'm making the effort to socialize and catch up with friends, we can only do so from our own homes, with our faces and voices emanating from little windows on devices. When I was on Zoom last week with an old friend on her phone, she walked "me" around her house, so "I" could say hello to her partner and kids who were all sheltering-in-place. Next time when I call "I" will get a tour of the concoctions her middle child has brought home and put in the fridge.

When I put myself into civic life or volunteer life, the entrances to domestic spaces are front and centre. I have an old sewing machine on which I'm learning to make bags for frontline health workers to put their dirty scrubs in at the end of the day, and as part of this effort, I went to pick up a bag of donated fabric from the home of the woman who co-ordinates the sewing team. She lives in my neighbourhood but I've never met her. I have, however, been in her backyard, hunting around for the key to her back shed where she left the fabric, so I don't have to come into contact with her. I was a bit worried the neighbours would see me and call the cops.

I don't usually root around in the private places of people I don't know, and even though my errand this time was virtuous, I had a tang of illicit self-awareness as I felt around under the paving stones for the key. When I found it, and let myself into the shed, I caught a glimpse of someone who must have been her standing in her kitchen, smiling and raising her hand to me in greeting from the other side of the window.

The next day I picked up a bag of donated blankets and bedding from one person's front door and drove it across the city, to the recipient's residence near my daughter's high school. The woman who was receiving the bedding buzzed me into her building and I walked up three flights of stairs, noticing dents in the walls and children's drawings and cooking smells. I left the grey canvas bag containing the things she would sleep on outside her door.

This experience might be like being a delivery person, one of the ubiquitous DoorDashers or SkipTheDishes couriers in masks and gloves, except that my pickups and deliveries happened outside the market where money is exchanged, or indeed, outside of any familiar framework other than a cobbled-together sort of civitas and mutual aid. Pandemic exigencies are drawing me into private domestic spaces I would never have visited in the before times, even as the radius of space that I travel as a worker or a person with an ordinary life shrinks down to my home, my grocery stores, my running route around a few blocks to King Edward Park and back, and my incursions into the river valley.

The Crash

Today while out on a socially distanced walk with a friend, we witnessed a motorcycle crash. A phalanx of revved-up bikers roared around a corner, one bike didn't make the turn, and bike and rider skidded off the road, hit a fence, bounced off, and collapsed on the ground, rider under the bike. For an instant, the out-of-control motorcycle looked to be heading straight at us, and my friend and I dove to the side to avoid it. We ran over to the crashed bike—the rider was struggling to get up but lucid and coherent. She couldn't put weight on one leg and she said she had struck her forehead, but a helmet and padding blunted most of the impact. I called 911, even though she insisted she was "hurt but not injured."

My friend and I waited for emergency services to arrive, and as we waited I segued into one of my crisis modes, spilling out warm and reassuring chatter about my own high-speed mishaps to draw down some of the panic I could see behind the eyes of the rider, who was clearly slipping into shock. My friend and I and the rest of the phalanx waited with the downed rider until the ambulance arrived and the professionals took over. And that is where the story should have ended.

But for the rest of the day I felt exhausted, apprehensive, and strangely fearful. Some of that may be down to the aftermath of an adrenaline surge, but I think the fearfulness was amped up by my awareness that this weekend was the official beginning of the re-launch into normalcy decreed by the province, on the advice of the chief medical officer of health. Cases appear to be going down. Stores are reopening and gatherings are recommencing, and judging by the state of parking lots, everybody's come out to play and shop.

I do not know if this re-launch should happen. I fear that in two weeks Covid cases will pick up after exposures on this holiday long weekend, and that at least a few of the gathering places will turn out to be virus hotspots. I felt some primitive resonance with the rider thrown from her motorcycle, who knew that she was hurt, but who insisted that she was not actually injured, and whose fear-based back-of-the-brain survival instinct was running high and loud. In my mind I see all of us, averting our eyes from the crash, trying to keep anxiety from tipping over into pain, and hoping against hope that the professionals are on their way to help us.

Summer 2020

On Trails

When I bought my condo about eight years ago, one of the selling features was access to the Mill Creek ravine portion of the river valley. I can take many paths into the ravine—down the stairs at the edge of the Faculté Saint-Jean playing fields, from the trailhead near the Peace Marker just off the upper parking lot for the outdoor pool, down the bike path switchbacks on the other side of Whyte just north of the fire station.

At the time I bought it and for some years afterwards, river valley access in my life functioned mainly as a sort of rhetorical token. I would tell people how great it was to be able to get into the valley so easily, how much I liked being close to the valley in the summer, and so forth. Deploying this token was also part of a half-intentional defensive strategy for having bought a place on the less fashionable east end of Whyte, away from the (expensive) Old Strathcona destination neighbourhoods. In reality, river valley access for me was like the Farmers' Market or the Fringe Festival, something I thought I ought to like because people like me like that sort of thing, but which was, in practical terms, more effort than I wanted to expend, most of the time.

Then Covid changed all that, among other things. I've spent more time tramping around the ravine in the last nine months than in the nine preceding years. I have favourite and less favourite paths, and I experience a visceral pull towards the trees and the water and the snow whenever the chaos of the human-made pandemic world is rising.

I've learned that the stretch of the ravine north of my place is honeycombed with mountain bike trails. These don't show up on official maps of the trail systems, and they come and go on the guerrilla crowd-sourced maps from apps like AllTrails and TrailForks, on which they bear cryptic names like DownTheFunWay or PipeDream or RootnRoll. They wind up and down, over hummocks and boulders, alarmingly close to the edge of bush-covered hillsides with ten-metre drop-offs, cutting across the official (wide, gravelled) trails, emerging into and out of denser bush of spruce, aspen or dogwood, depending on location. Mountain bikers have left signs of their habitation, in the form of narrow little bridges of rough slats across gullies, or signs nailed to trees inviting travellers to "share, respect, enjoy."

The trails are not efficient ways to get from one place to another. The straightest distance between two points is not the point, the point is to mark out a narrow space (slightly wider than a fat-bike tire) that twists and turns and ideally gains and loses lots of elevation.

I would never have known of the existence of these trails if I hadn't walked off the official paths. I might never have seen them if I only ventured into the ravine in the best weather of the summer. Mud or snow show the imprints of big mountain-bike tires, and once my eye became attuned to these tracks, I could see the trail taking shape. I can't really navigate them without the aid of trekking poles to anchor me as I slide down inclines or to pull me up over tangles of roots embedded in a slippery hillside. These are not very pedestrian-friendly trails, and more than once I've determined that if I continued any further I would be at risk of sliding down straight into the creek, and turned back.

On these trails, I'm always in danger of being crushed by a mountain biker coming up on me suddenly. Some are diligent about calling out "On your left!"; others are more diligent about grunting and swearing at obstacles. Mountain bikers have the right to be there, certainly, but these trails are not their property. Anyone who is able to push their way off the official bike paths and into terra incognita belongs to this place.

What Are You Looking At?

Two days ago I was waiting for the bus. Public transport is free during the pandemic, and even as the outside world lurches back towards normality, the buses, with "please board at the back" signs and yellow tape marking off alternating rows of seats, are an ambulatory reminder that we are not yet back in normal times. These visual cues play on my pandemic-awareness, so I find myself "masking up" to board the bus, even though I know the risk of either contracting or transmitting a virus on a fifteen-minute ride down Whyte Avenue is negligible.

So I was primed for virus-awareness, homemade mask in place and feeling good about it, at the bus stop. A pickup truck pulled to my side of the street and the occupants started hollering at me. The content of the holler was unintelligible—presumably, the limited vocabulary of the street hassle—but the gestures, hands waving around their faces and pointing at mine, made it clear that my mask had caught their attention and they wanted me to know they thought it was stupid. The truck occupants were an unfortunate Alberta cliché come to life—large young-ish white men with dirty baseball caps and half-beards in mismatched camouflage jackets. I responded with a middle finger; they hollered again and one of them smacked the door panel for emphasis, and then the light changed and they drove off.

I thought about this unwanted encounter. On the one hand, this is generic harassment. Any woman or any person of colour existing in public has encountered some version of these yahoos. This has happened before. On the other hand, populist rage is the flavour of the times, and maybe that's what I was seeing: Trump-ish resentment and hostility towards the effete city-dwellers who want everyone to play safe and listen to the educated people who tell us to cover our faces.

And on the other hand, starting to run out of hands—what did those men think they were doing? I don't mean that I want to examine their thoughts in a false-consciousness, discursively-determined, political-analytical sense. I mean that if I could have frozen the moment, somehow induced a calming spell to fall over everyone, and asked them: "Why are you doing that? What is the outcome you're aiming towards by hollering at the middle-aged woman in a face mask? What do you see?"—what would they have said?

On the surface (I almost wrote "on the face of it") yelling at people in masks makes no sense. My mask has no impact on the freedom of action or movement available to them. I am not attempting to obstruct them. Nothing is being enforced. If they want to drive around in a pickup truck with bare faces, my mask-wearing presents no obstacle. You do you.

What if I had acceded to the anti-mask hollering and taken my own mask off? Would I have gotten applause and thumbs up? Would any change in my behaviour, any acknowledgement of the legitimacy of their views, be a satisfying conclusion to this episode, from their point of view? Or is yelling at women at bus stops an end in itself, and the mask/no mask, safety/liberty argument simply the name of the discharge valve through which this perpetual hostility escapes?

These are empirical questions, not rhetorical ones. I wish that I could step into some sort of discursive neutral zone and ask them. I wish I could ask the protestors in Detroit whom I've read about, who tried to block hospital emergency parking bays and keep the ambulances from getting in or out—what is the nature of the thing that you are attempting to achieve? If you were successful and stopped the ER from admitting any new patients, why would that success matter? If we step away from the assumption that behaviour like this is purely theatrical and step into the assumption that this is behaviour that is meant to be instrumental, to achieve something, what would we learn?

At this point in the pandemic, I am surrounded by evidence of public behaviour that seems to me to be completely irrational, much of it triggered by people's choices about what kind of protective measures to take, or people's choices to acknowledge that the virus is real and dangerous. I can explain this behaviour by using concepts like patriarchy, neoliberalism, white supremacy and class ressentiment, and I think these explanations work, in the sense that they are both adequately prescriptive and descriptive, but I also want to know what's going on in the minds of the people who are blocking the ambulances and harassing the Costco clerks and filling up the internet with anti-WHO screeds and hollering at bus stops. What are you attempting to achieve? Why the fuck you yelling at me, buddy?

Twice-Blooming Lilacs

Lilacs are blooming as the city greens up after late-spring rains. The first time I noticed them as I headed down the steps into the river valley near the Faculté Saint-Jean, I thought, "How odd. Lilacs blossoming twice in one year. Strange that I haven't noticed this before." Then I thought some more. How could the lilacs bloom twice? It's still the spring. Not enough time has elapsed since winter for the lilac bushes to bud, flower, die back and bud again.

So why this sense of déjà vu? I've had so many experiences of uncanny feelings recently that they're really starting to bother me, so I dug deep into memory to figure out why this looked like something I'd already seen this year. I realized that I had in fact seen lilacs earlier in 2020, but that was in Ottawa, in the second week in March. I spent two days walking in a vast circle around my hotel, just as the gate was coming down on shelter-in-place and stay-at-home orders and just before I returned to Edmonton, shaken by the weirdness of what was starting to happen. For reasons best known to my unconscious, I had transposed Ottawa and Edmonton and ascribed lilacs in March to the wrong city.

Okay, but wait a minute. Lilacs, in Ottawa, in March? I also remember that there was snow on the ground, and that I wished I had brought warmer gloves. Shouldn't that be too cold for lilac bushes to flower?

After googling "when do lilacs bloom," I realized that it was not possible for me to have seen them in Ottawa. They don't come into flower anywhere in Canada before May. My memory of seeing them in Ottawa was a confabulation, devised by some part of me to provide an explanation for the feeling of seeing-for-the-second-time that I experienced here in Edmonton, in June, walking around my neighbourhood. But I was not, could not have been, seeing them for a second time. The recognition I'm experiencing now is not really recognition.

Things were becoming even more uncanny. I was getting a little obsessed by this question of lilacs. More googling led to neurological and psychoanalytic explanations for the phenomenon of déjà vu (a glitch in the wiring of short-term and long-term memory, leading to the sensation that a memory is being retrieved when it is actually being created in the moment; an unacknowledged wish-fulfillment; a sign of temporal lobe disorders). Any or all could be true.

But what it felt like was a disorder of time. The months seemed to have stretched out for years, long enough for natural cycles to repeat. Nothing is happening "in good time." The temporal rhythms of work and leisure have been stilled, anticipated dates in the future— holidays, meetings, travel—have disappeared. Events that happened before Covid belong to another age. Living through an epidemic that is unprecedented means living through an epidemic that has no knowable future, only guesses, and a radically shortened time horizon. "We're going day by day," which I heard constantly in the early weeks, is not only a description of making do and improvising ways around this new normal, it's also a statement about how time has changed.

So, an endless spring in Edmonton, plenty of time for lilacs to bloom twice. Why not? Or lilacs in March in Ottawa, their flowering accelerated to coexist with the slush and snow of late winter. Why not? I am struggling to articulate something about pandemic time that makes déjà vu experiences and unreliable memories seem not only plausible but also unexceptional. (I did not for a moment worry that I had temporal lobe epilepsy or some inexpressible psychic conflict worming its way out. I thought, "well, it's the pandemic. That explains it.")

The pandemic distorts the perception of time, which distorts memory, which ultimately distorts selfhood. Who am I in the pandemic? The answer, in part: someone who's gotten a bit lost in time.

Curiosity Cabinet

According to his biographer Nicholas Shakespeare, the British travel writer Bruce Chatwin's grandmother had a cabinet of curiosities that fascinated the young writer. The cabinet was a late-Victorian assemblage of exotica, bits of human artifact and the natural world, preserved under glass because they came from places that were far away, set apart from Chatwin's mundane life in Birmingham in the 1940s.

This afternoon I was clearing out cupboards in my bathroom. I realized that over the past decade, I had unintentionally curated a sort of accidental curiosity cabinet on a pandemic theme. This collection predates Covid, but it comes from a moment when I anticipated the anxieties of the pandemic. It consists of debris from previous global health emergencies, when I had feared that The Big One might be about to fall on us. This flotsam calls up a curiosity cabinet of pandemic futures foretold, each item referencing moments years ago, which turned out to be only rehearsals for 2020, moments when I thought, "no need to panic, but this might get really bad."

- A packet of five N95 respirator masks dating back to the SARS outbreak in 2003. In hindsight, this seems like a mini-crisis, a pandemic-lite, which claimed about 800 lives, less than that daily body count in the US during April and May. To purchase these masks, I went to a medical supply store and tried to explain that I didn't want standard surgical masks. The clerk hadn't heard of them—"N95" had not yet become a familiar term—but eventually found a dust-covered box labelled entirely in Chinese but bearing the 3M logo and the term "N95."
- A box of blue latex surgical gloves from 2005, the year that I served on the medical ethics subcommittee of the city of Edmonton's pandemic preparedness committee, which had been set up in the wake of SARS.

As part of the subcommittee, I read histories of the 1918 influenza and discussed what principles should govern the allocation of ventilators and negative-pressure hospital rooms. It all seemed sombre and dystopian at the time, but just barely real enough for me to start thinking that it might be wise to avoid hospitals altogether if or when The Big One arrived. I was strongly impressed by the idea that if The Big One was big enough, people who were admitted to hospital might not be allowed to leave. This led me to think that I needed to be able to control infection and fever at home, that there might come a time when medical care was not safe. I imagined myself barricaded inside with my daughter, trying to rig up some form of isolation.

- A temperature-gun thermometer, also SARS-era.
- A box of disposable medical masks, ubiquitous in 2020, dating from the H1N1 outbreak in 2009.
- A ten-day course of azithromycin, prescribed just-in-case as malaria therapy before a trip to Africa in 2008, still in the bathroom cupboard, saved for a time when someone in my household might be really sick with a bacterial infection but going to the hospital would be out of the question.
- A ten-day course of ciprofloxacin from an African trip a few years later, ditto.
- A bottle of isopropyl alcohol and a box of long sleeve-length rubber gloves from the first Ebola cases in north America, circa 2014.
- Packets of oral rehydration salts, dating from some time around the turn of the century, excavated and stashed in the cupboard because of Ebola.

And then we get into the current emergency:

- Several bottles of hydrogen peroxide and isopropyl from beautician supply stores, just before the "purchases limited" signs went up. Black latex gloves, same.

- At least half a dozen jars of aloe vera gel, which I read on the internet could be combined with the peroxide or the isopropyl to make hand sanitizer, at a time at the beginning of the pandemic when commercial sanitizer was limited to tiny bottles at check-out desks limited to one per customer, assuming you could find it at all. I ordered most of the aloe vera online from an outfit in China, which was trying to simulate The Body Shop in logo and lettering. I now have a lifetime supply of aloe vera gel.
- A box of disposable surgical masks, at the exorbitant cost of $50 for 50, which I heard about through a sort of social media samizdat, and drove out to the deep southwest of the city to buy from a narrow shop in a strip mall with a hand-lettered sign in the window advertising same. I must have looked aghast at the price because the proprietor told me solemnly, "these are very valuable and you're going to be glad you've got them when you really need them." So far that has not happened.
- Airplane-sized bottles of hand sanitizer and disinfectant gel, bought for trips over the years to places where the water was dubious. Never used, scattered in various drawers and now con-solidated into one supply.
- Heavy-duty antipyretics including Tylenol-3s and codeine-laced paracetamols, prescribed and otherwise, hoarded against a day when someone in my household might spike a dangerously high fever at a time when hospitals were off limits (see above con-cerning latex gloves).
- Five KN95 masks ordered from China in March (the knockoff version of N95).
- Ten more genuine N95s, which arrived weeks after I had for-gotten I'd ordered them, sourced from a small business in Vancouver that I sometimes bought clothes from, which had "a connection" in the Emirates.

I couldn't decide what to do with these curiosities. Reorganize them, stuff them back into the cupboard, lay them out in a glass-fronted cabinet with a hand-lettered placard labelled "Global health imagination"? They were evidence of the years during which I had known, or had suspected, that something really bad might be coming, knowledge that I had managed to suppress or set aside most of the time, except for the intermittent bursts of awareness of SARS or Ebola or MERS or H1N1 or multi-drug-resistant superbugs or Ebola again.

When I imagined the day that I might need to mix the rehydration salts, or break open the masks or uncap the long-expired antibiotics courses, I imagined it apocalyptic and dramatic and removed from everyday life. I did not imagine that it would be an ordinary day, or a succession of ordinary days, or that I would be occupying myself by cleaning out cupboards and making up stories about the contents, while The Big One moved forward, quietly and inexorably, all around me.

All the Futures

As the pandemic proceeds through numbered opening-up stages, the future is fracturing into a spectrum of divergent times-after, like the Pink Floyd album cover with one ray of blackness going into a prism and seven colours going out. First there was "we're all in this together," with a collective holding of breath and a radical levelling of public experience. Everything was shut down, everybody was home, the streets were uniformly empty, and no one knew what was coming. We shared the stasis, time stopping in the moment after the gate came down or the door slammed shut or whatever metaphor you prefer for the middle of March.

Now our futures look different. Back-to-work is real for many people, retail is open, recreation is soon to follow, and it looks to me like some futures will proceed more or less as they were before, albeit punctuated by the pandemic. There's a rush hour once again, the malls are open until eight, and construction of the new southeast LRT line is back on track, literally.

But for other people—students, teachers, performers, clergy, coaches—the future looks like an eternal virus-now. Anyone whose livelihood depends (or depended) on medium-to-large groups of people engaged in co-ordinated activities in the same physical space is grappling with the disappearance of that space, and realizing that the withdrawal from normal that began in March is going to last an indefinitely long time.

I'm struck by the extent to which I as a textbook introvert had built a life out of being part of groups of people engaged in co-ordinated activities in public space. That describes teaching and a lot of research activities, it describes church functions, it describes the volunteer work I did and the youth sports functions that took up my weekends. Now that's gone. The space has shrunk down to the size of this laptop screen and the people have lost their bodies and become two-dimensional heads in a three-inch square, sometimes with eye-catching domestic events in the tiny background. And I don't know if or when that's going to change.

I'm fortunate that my pandemic future probably does not include losing my job or going broke or deteriorating mental health. I'm resourceful by nature, and I have resources. But I think I'm going to experience (even more) cognitive dissonance between a future of crisis-driven change to just about everything I value, and the apparent business-as-usual future unfolding around me. I'm guessing this will peak around September, when the cyclical rhythms of the academic schedule, which have structured my years since the turn of the century, move towards the annual return to the classroom. Except this year, the future is going to diverge.

I'm also aware that business-as-usual could be evanescent, and the arrival of a second wave of infection could flip everything back to Pandemic Time Zero. So many places have already veered off onto a dystopian timeline—Houston, Miami, the Four Corners of the southwestern

United States, upstate New York, all of Brazil. I have entirely unmerited luck, to be where I am, doing what I do, whatever that will turn out to be.

Here's a slightly embarrassing pop-culture elision: in the last episode of the science-fiction TV show *Angel*, the band of heroes is cornered by a towering mob of demons, the odds are against them, and they don't know if they'll survive. "...In terms of a plan?" asks one. "Let's get to work," says the titular character, drawing a sword. Cut to black. So unsatisfying, as an ending. What happens next? There was a plan, there was no plan, they all die, a few survive, they vanquish the horde? In Covid time, I don't think anyone has a sword or a plan, and we can't quite see where the demons are or what happens after the cut to black. What can we do? Pick up whatever we've got, and get to work.

The Licence Plate

Another strange time-stretching-out moment this evening: I glanced at my licence plate and thought "oh hell, I forgot to renew my registration. I'm missing this year's sticker. I'd better take care of that before I get a fine." But I am not missing this year's sticker. Stickers are good for twelve months. I have a sticker dated November 2019 and I was looking directly at it when the thought ran through my mind. On some level below consciousness, I registered "November 2019" as "long, long, long ago, and therefore a problem," rather than "in the adequately recent past, and therefore nothing to see here, move along." I had to stop for a moment and do the math. November 2019 was seven months ago, it is now June 2020 and I have five more months until the registration expires. No, it has not been over a year since I last paid a registration fee.

The way time feels now—its elasticity, its density, the sense of the recent past as far away—is not the way the calendar works. I can't rely on my felt sense of how near or how far I am from a point in the past. Spatial metaphors for time have become pretty much useless, because I can't feel the distance anymore. It's only been seven months since I renewed my registration; 2019 is not impossibly far away. It is not a tiny spot way off in the horizon of the past.

Bewildered

Portentous words: I woke up this morning with the thought that "bewilderment" is related to "wild" and "wilderness." And indeed, I was right, according to the Oxford English Dictionary. To be bewildered, disoriented, confused, uncertain is to be surrounded by wild things. I am bewildered.

    I am spending more and more of my time with wild things during the pandemic. I'm often down in the river valley, where wild things grow. I hear reports of coyotes and moose, but haven't seen anything bigger than a hare crossing my path. The wild things that stay in one place are becoming more familiar to me—the trees, flowers, bushes and shrubs that grow randomly. How did I live here for twenty years without knowing any of their names? I could distinguish a conifer from a deciduous tree and could recognize a few of the more obvious flowers, like daisies and dandelions, but I had neither the words to name nor the eyes to see the great bounty of wild vegetation.

    I downloaded two plant-identification apps to my phone and started learning names. Some names, especially those of smallish flowers, were redolent of old English ballads, yarrow and tansy and mallow and burdock and campion and larkspur. I heard Steeleye Span and Fairport Convention when I first saw those names, and I was reminded of the hold that the colonizing British have on the settler imagination, more than two centuries after they came out here and started naming things. Their words overwrote all the other names the river valley plants might have carried in Indigenous languages, at least in the official sources, pulling the North Saskatchewan valley into the orbit of Europe. The dogwood, or osier, for example, which clusters along the edges of the paths, waist-high with spotted white berries. The name has nothing to do with dogs: it comes from the same root as "dagger," referring to the shape of the leaves, and was incorporated into English from Danish some time before the thirteenth century.

I'd been reading Robin Wall Kimmerer's *Braiding Sweetgrass*, in which she calls the plants of Oklahoma and upstate New York by their Indigenous names. I tried to find a source for Cree names for tansy and campion and their companions but didn't succeed. Instead, I discovered the works of Robert Dale Rogers, an Edmonton herbalist who self-published guides to the medicinal and other properties of river valley plants. I didn't have much luck using his books to identify plants—his pictures showed plants at the peak of their flowering or fruiting, which didn't correspond to the times when I was wandering around looking at them—but I did learn that the bark of the ubiquitous chokecherry can be boiled down into a cough syrup, and that the root of the tiny Solomon's seal can be used for birth control. How exactly this worked was not explained.

My favourite was burdock, a weed that started small and grew alarmingly quickly, teeming on the riverbanks. By midsummer its burrs were at my eye level. The flower of the burdock starts off as a globe covered with hundreds of tiny spikes, swelling gradually over a period of weeks until it bursts, revealing a brilliant purple and crimson blossom inside. The spiky carapace, which contains the seeds of the burdock, is said to have inspired George de Mestral, the Swiss inventor of Velcro, when he tried in vain to detach the burrs from his dog. Burdock burrs and flowers are so precise and so detailed in their adhesive spininess that they look like objects to serve as scientific models of something, not random effusions of plant growth.

I was nose to spike with a burdock plant in Dawson Park, gaze fixed on the pointy tips attached to the spherical body, when I understood why I found them fascinating. The globe-and-spike pattern looked like the standard model of the coronavirus itself, with the now-famous spike proteins attached to the round envelope containing the RNA that highjacks human cells into reproducing the viral invader. Burdock was a reminder of the reason why I was down here in the valley in the first place, instead of somewhere else that had people around. Seeing the virus anatomy in benign botanical form was uncanny, a reminder that even when I was surrounded by flowers and trees and water and soil, the pandemic had its tenacious Velcro grip on my imagination.

Covid Anxiety

I had my first episode of what I think is Covid anxiety yesterday. My daughter and I had gone out to pick up supplies from a crafts supply store. We'd done an online click-and-collect purchase, but when we got to the store to collect, my daughter wanted to go in to look for a particular type of drawing pen. No problem, I said. We went in and found the pens. There was a long lineup for the registers. We joined the line.

Within a couple of minutes, I started feeling lightheaded and vertigo-y, and possessed by a profound desire to get out before an unspecified bad thing happened. I've had "anxiety issues" in the past, of the subclinical variety, so I knew what was going on. I was not going to die or fall victim to a bad thing, I was just a bit—triggered.

Why there and then, and not other times in other stores or public spaces? Here's what I think:

We were in a checkout line. This means that movement is necessarily restricted—it's not proper social etiquette to meander back and forth or leave and wander and rejoin the line, unless you are an extremely young child (of course, I could have bolted, but there were many countervailing forces inducing me not to bolt). If you're in a suggestible state, a circumstance in which you're constrained from moving around can feel like being trapped, even though you're not trapped, and nothing other than convention is requiring you to stay.

I didn't have my mask with me (because the plan was to pick up an online order, not wander around aisles looking for pens). So I didn't have the option for minor and inconspicuous action to dial down anxiety that fiddling with a mask would have provided.

At the best of times, I do not enjoy big-box stores full of unhappy parents. The ambient tension generated by suburban moms snapping not-very-quietly at whiny children was grating on me. I was stuck in an aquarium of Karens, which I didn't much like, plus the possibility of the virus, which I profoundly didn't like.

What was going on here? Why did a trip to the craft store set off this jangling? I think it happened because once again, Covid was bringing me back around to previous dispositions, feelings and sensations that properly belong in the past.

The catalyst was that day's news. I'd just been reading news on my phone about hospitalizations taking off in Texas, Florida and California. I lived in Texas as a child, in what is now a sprawling exurb of Houston. My mental-image association for Texas is acres of asphalt and generic overly bright big stores in commercial precincts that seemed, to a child, to go on forever. This somewhat bleak retail-scape was where I now found myself in real life.

My best dial-it-down strategy for anxiety involves slow, deep, mindful breaths. Unfortunately, this means exhaling a lot. So in addition to the above, I had to worry whether people around me noticed that I was breathing very...decisively, and whether they were interpreting this as an infection risk and getting nervous about me. I was thinking too much about what I was feeling, and was thinking about what other people might be thinking about the ways I was feeling, and this nervous conjunction of projection into other people's minds plus anticipation of eye-rolls or other signs of disapproval built up in me a feedback loop of anticipatory anxiety.

In the event, nothing bad happened, as I knew nothing would. After a few minutes we were at the front of the line, we paid, and got out, and I felt better as soon as I got a full lungful of outside air.

The incident wasn't forgotten, however. I fretted about it: "Oh hell, not this again. I want to get through the rest of this pandemic without the hamster wheel of weird and pointlessly trivial anxiety episodes.

I do not want yet another random element to complicate all the complicated calculations that are already spinning around as I try to calibrate my life to a global health crisis. And I absolutely do not want to worry about what might happen if I leave home."

So far, so good. I've had no more anxiety, and I'm optimistic that the power of the Craft Supply Incident has been neutralized by figuring out the "why" of the Craft Supply Incident, as in "why then, why there?" Analytical thought is my go-to in most distressing situations, and it may have helped me here.

Downward

In the last few weeks, I've heard about several friends and acquaintances who are going into tailspins. The particulars don't really matter; the common trajectory is what's remarkable. I'm of an age at which reports of midlife crises often arrive, dispatches from the cliché front: substance abuse, dissipation, wildly inappropriate interpersonal behaviour, dramatic renunciations, outbursts of narcissism and staying in bed all day.

However, the reports I get during these pandemic days are not all from the usual suspects for such crises—the people who are prone to drama and misadventure—and the speed and trajectory of their fall seems to be sharper. Reading the news from the wider world outside my own networks tells me that this is not something unique to my social bubble, that many people are losing altitude and pressure rapidly, veering off toward the ground. It's happening in the province of Alberta, it's happening at national levels, it's happening with famous people that I sort of know about. The centre's not holding anywhere.

These tailspins are disturbing. They hit me harder than they would have during the non-pandemic times. The hit is not just the jolt of empathy for someone who's going through a hard time, it's a shock with a minor note of dread. What's going on? Why are these lives falling apart?

And of course, am I next? I brood over them and catalogue a range of emotional reactions, from compassion to outrage to cynicism and back.

The speed and pitch of the tailspins must be related to the heightened stresses of the pandemic. Death tolls are mounting, and sane and sober voices in the US are talking of one hundred thousand new cases a day coming soon, something I could not have imagined forty or sixty days ago. Just today, the rolling seven-day average for new cases in the US reached a record high for the twenty-seventh day in a row. There is nothing but badness.

When I read about the billowing growth of the pandemic and when I get real-time text or social media bulletins about some acquaintance combusting, the same thoughts occur. In both situations, I keep thinking, "Well, it can't get worse than this. There's a limit somewhere. Things can't get any more awful. Oh wait, yes they can and they just did." This idea of free-fall—that people are going to get worse and worse, not just in a medical state-of-the-body sense but in a state-of-the-soul sense, in a staying-in-bed-longer-and-longer sense, in a crazily-wrong-words-and-deeds sense—is destabilizing.

When will these people hit the ground and stop falling? What if there is no ground to hit?

Crime and Punishment/Everything Is Free

In the June 29th issue of the *New Yorker*, there's a hybrid book review/personal essay by David Denby about re-reading *Crime and Punishment*. I read it in high school a million years ago and had forgotten it ends with Raskolnikov in prison in Siberia, dreaming of a plague. Denby quotes:

> Entire settlements, entire cities and nations would be infected and go mad. Everyone became anxious and no one understood anyone else, each thought the truth was contained in himself·

alone, and suffered looking at others, beat his breast, wept and wrung his hands. They did not know whom or how to judge, could not agree on what to regard as evil, what as good. They did not know whom to accuse, whom to vindicate.

Well, obviously that resonates strongly for Denby in 2020, writing more than a hundred days into our own plague with apocalyptic tendencies. But he is astute enough to say that the deepest parallels with *Crime and Punishment* are not in the fever dreams at the end of the book but in Dostoevsky's depiction of St. Petersburg.

This is the sort of city that fired the deeply pessimistic European imaginations of the founders of my own discipline, sociology. The city is rootless and purposeless, filled with people who have been displaced from the middle classes, whose claims on living space and work are precarious and tenuous. They turn their experience of loss into jealousy and anxiety about other people, fuelled by gossip. At the risk of sounding like a B+ student in Intro to Literature, it's no surprise that the central murder victim in *Crime and Punishment* is a pawnbroker— her work is to take away even the little fragments that her neighbours have managed to hold onto. And of course, there's sickness in St. Petersburg—cholera and water-borne diseases, in this case.

Reading Denby's essay reminded me how much of Dostoevsky's novel is about things that are taken away. I started thinking about what it's like to live through a period when things are taken away.

I should be clear that I don't mean just things that have been taken away from me as an individual. My office at work, plans for travel, some face-to-face interactions—these have been taken away. In my world these are not trivial matters, but they aren't terrible ones either. I still have a job, a home, a future. Nonetheless, I've spent the last few months watching things go away and seeing bitterness rise up in the spaces left behind.

School went away. Summer camp went away. Public space went away. Private retail space went away. And the jobs and security and order that these things created went away too. For a few months, there was no rush hour on the main thoroughfare where I live, and even now if I'm out on my balcony on a weekend, as I am today, I sense pauses of five, ten or even fifteen seconds of no traffic at all.

Some of it has come part of the way back, through cautious and hold-your-breath re-openings, but the anxiety and confusion of Raskolnikov's fever dream has come with them. (And for the record "cautious" and "hold-your-breath" is exactly how I think re-openings should happen, so this is not a complaint). Seventy thousand new cases in the US today. Images that would not be out of place in the hallucinatory sequences of bleak Russian novels have gone viral (as they say)—respectable burghers with guns driving off the rabble, out-breaks of crazy prophecy in the market square or Costco, and leaders entranced by a world-denying millenarian vision of political triumph that requires the sacrifice of an uncountable number of people.

But I digress. In my lifeworld bubble in Edmonton, I sometimes experience things-going-away as strangely tranquil, renunciatory with-out the pain. Many of the compulsions that kept me disciplined have fallen off the cliff—professional obligations to write more and teach more and get more grants and go to more meetings, the drive to self-improvement that was enacted through technologies of betterment like group classes and civic commitments and academic rituals formal and informal, with attendant fear-of-missing-out—it all just went away. I see people one at a time if I see them at all; I'm writing and preparing lectures for the fall, but no one is really paying attention to what I'm doing. I'm not having a crisis of meaning or identity because I still think my work is worth doing, but I'm conscious that nobody's watching. I'm staying home because there's not really anything else to do. It all went away.

This is not exactly relaxing or soothing. It's more like being a bit dazed, but still awake and observant. Cressida Heyes, in her 2020 book *Anaesthetics of Existence*, describes what she calls anaesthetic time—periods when the normative movement of life towards the future is stilled, and individuals inhabit a sort of non-linear drift through time, often associated with syncope or depressant intoxication (although, as I am discovering, it's possible to be fully conscious and sober and still a bit anaesthetized by pandemic time). And as something to be on the inside of, pandemic renunciatory calm beats pandemic anxiety or pandemic rage.

Since I became aware of how it feels when everything-went-away, I've had the lyrics of a Gillian Welch song, "Everything Is Free," running through my head. It's a dreamy lyric about someone, a singer, for whom the structures of world and work have just...gone. She muses about maybe getting some money from the tip jar in the bar, maybe putting some gas in the car, but decides not to. She's not performing anymore. She's staying home. Might sing a little bit for herself, might not. She doesn't mind hard work, but for now, it's come to a stop. "Free" in the title takes two meanings: her work is free, because she gives it away, but it's also free in the sense that life has, somehow, become unstructured.

I looked up the history of this song, and because I always want to believe that people I admire think exactly like me, I was a bit disappointed to learn that it was about the impact on artists of the first internet streaming services in the 1990s, rather than about my own existential oddness. But it still stays with me—drifting along inside my head, a strangely calm counterpoint to Raskolnikov's fevered dream of the plague.

Objects

My relationship to things is changing, and by things I mean objects, inanimate stuff that has weight and mass and materiality and extension. Chairs, books, fruits, houseplants. With the things that I like, I experience an absurdly heightened cathexis, a concentration of attention and appreciation more intense than anything since childhood, when I would become fixated on wanting or needing that one specific book or toy. The excitement generated by these objects feels a bit excessive. Library books, for instance—the knowledge that I have a really good book, that there's a reading experience waiting for me that is going to be *so good*—that anticipation is more visceral than it was pre-pandemic, when the anticipation of a new book was only one of many anticipations of things that might happen. Similarly, discovering that my bread machine still works. It's an *amazing machine,* the things it can do! Dinner rolls! Fruit breads! I'm not likely to make any of them, but I'm in the presence of wonder when I contemplate it.

This is where I find myself enacting one of the new clichés of the pandemic, the devotion to hobbies, crafts, the slightly frenetic makings of things. So far I've cycled through sewing (my first sewing machine! I can make masks and upcycle my clothes!), kombucha-making (I got a scoby from a friend and it is *so cool* to listen to the tiny fizzes as it ferments!), and devotion to houseplants (coffee grounds in the bottom of the pot means the aloes drain better!). I wonder whether these activities are those of an adult being purposeful and creative under pressure, or more akin to a nine-year-old playing obsessively with Lego and My Little Pony to distract herself from parents fighting about the overdue bills.

They are definitely a deflection of something. These intensified feelings about things are not born of need, or yearning, or even superficial desire for stuff. At the moment, there's really nothing I need that I don't have, and if I'm honest, not many things that I actually desperately want. Instead, this intensity about objects is filling the mental spaces where other people used to be.

Out of an abundance of caution my household has become insular, or perhaps peninsular, with a few strands of land still connecting us to the greater mass of humankind. Even pre-Covid, I wasn't exactly wildly gregarious, by choice and by temperament; and now, also by choice, face-to-face interactions have withdrawn from my repertoire, and in their place I seem to find mangoes really captivating. Or hiking boots. Or a coffee press. If this keeps up, I'm going to approximate the mythical Zen adepts who spend half an hour contemplating a raisin before eating it, except that my state has nothing spiritual about it. It's a psychic artifact of an unprecedented set of social constraints.

I don't think this is anthropomorphizing, as I'm not ascribing personalities where personality does not exist. I don't feel like I'm starving for human contact and making do by pretending a lavender plant is my friend. I just seem to have more capacity *to be aware*, and to be directing it towards the objects that have been around me all the time, but that pre-Covid were faded out by the constant buzz of human interaction. Now the buzz has quieted, but somehow my listening, my attentiveness, has remained.

Where Is Here and Where Is There?

The pandemic is messing with my sense of place as well as time. By "place" I don't mean topography (for instance, the fact that I'm writing this in the Bonnie Doon Community League Park as opposed to Casablanca). I mean the building blocks of spatial awareness, of what is here and what is there; what is near and what is far.

The Great Withdrawal may have sucked people out of public spaces, but the public parts of my own life—my work and volunteer commitments—didn't stop. They just came home. Feminists have deconstructed the myth of a public/private divide forever, so the idea that work was home and home was work was not new to me. It was just intensified by the pandemic.

But the technologies on which I rapidly became utterly dependent had a treacherous effect on my ability to sense what was where, or more precisely, who was where. It's not a new insight, the idea that technology has shrunk or collapsed the distances separating people, starting with those century-old inventions with the ubiquitous prefix tele-, like the -gram and the -phone, and ending with Zoom 2020, in which tele- is so obvious it doesn't bear mentioning.

However, my experience was not that distances had shrunk but that they had gone away entirely. In normal times I had Skyped with colleagues, but I usually had a visceral sense that the other person was somewhere else, somewhere not-here. I had this sense because I had met them in their place of work (or mine), or at church, or at a conference, or in someone's home, or in some other location where we had physically overlapped in real time.

But during Covid, I am encountering and interacting with people whom I have never met off the screen, and so I can't place them anywhere other than on the screen. The screen is in my bedroom, as am I, for up to twenty hours each day. In my bedroom there appeared, over the past six months, several completely new acquaintances, including an American anthropologist whose grandparents had been friends with mine, an Australian global health expert who collected Covid diaries, nine of my oldest friends from high school (displayed as a panel of nine squares, like the Brady Bunch) and a reunion of over sixty people who had been staff at the summer camp I had worked at in the 1980s, which derailed slightly because we hadn't figured out that if we all sing campfire songs at once, the Zoom feedback produces yowls.

Where were these people, really? In theory, they were in southeastern Illinois, in Queensland, in The Hague, and so forth. But I had no experience of them being anywhere except very close, sharing the same oversized IKEA armchair and jury-rigged laptop apparatus. Meanwhile, people who had been materially, corporeally, topographically close to me before Covid, people I might see at work or in the course of other local commitments in Edmonton, either receded into that same screen or decorporealized themselves even further, turning into emails or text messages or nothing at all.

After several weeks of not seeing real people in real time, the people I knew in Edmonton started to seem vaporous or insubstantial, as though they too didn't have a physical place to which I could pin them in my mental cartography. They seemed very distant, at risk of vanishing entirely into the mist. My mental map of who is where—this person is in the neighbourhood, that one is in Tanzania—dried up and shrivelled and blew away. Maps, mental and otherwise, aren't very useful when there is here and here is there. No one is closer to me, or further from me, than the little figures in boxes on my screen.

The End of Science World

I have moved in and out of various faiths, but I have always believed in Good Science. In this way as in others, I am an Enlightenment subject, certain that there is reality independent of my perceptions (or my existence), that it is knowable, and that the application of correct methods will produce knowledge that can be used to change reality. I believe in empirical observation, the testing of falsifiable hypotheses, and the randomized controlled trial.

My own scholarly work does not usually involve falsifiable hypotheses and randomized controlled trials—in my sociological and historical research, I have generally operated along the lines of "here's something interesting, I wonder what I can say about it?" Nonetheless, when it comes to authoritative statements about how things work, especially biological things like viruses, I live in Science World.

I know not everyone lives in Science World. Many people live in what I think of as Enchanted World, thanks to Canadian philosopher Charles Taylor's *A Secular Age*, where transcendent intelligences make things happen, and powers and principalities move the furniture every now and then. I'd include religious fundamentalists in this group, along with spiritual-but-not-religious New Age types and the generally superstitious. I realize that the distinction between Science World and Magic World is more one of circumstance than of quality (and am indeed supposed to be working on an academic paper making the not very original argument that Magic World is real in its consequences for motivating individual action and constructing explanations for why and how events happen). Even if the distinction between Science World and Magic World is sometimes shaky, I still subscribe to that distinction, and to the idea that everybody is a citizen of one or the other, and most of us hold passports for both.

But Covid denialism, and Covid anti-science in general, is challenging me in a way that religious beliefs or other forms of faith in the supernatural never did. I am realizing that there are people out there who not only reject scientific explanations for the virus or for the particular shape of the pandemic, but who also do not have a replacement episteme. They aren't saying the pandemic is "part of God's plan," or "cosmic vibrations" or "collective unconscious" or whatever. It's just— no, no, no. Deny, deny, deny. There is no virus, nobody is getting sick, no one has really died of it, nobody needs a mask, no to this, no to that, no to everything and yes to nothing.

In the flares of rage and craziness, especially but not only in the US with its Trump madness, I see not just Science World and Magic World, but also tear-it-all-down Denial World, but without an accompanying affirmation of anything else. How do I explain the people burning masks for no apparent reason except to oppose mask mandates, or throwing Covid parties, or threatening nurses and medical staff because...why? No coherent answer emerges, except that they're all angry and it's all bullshit, whatever that means.

I'm not averse to nonrational ways of experiencing the world. I'm really interested in how people with profound religious convictions go through life, people whose ontologies pivot on the substance of things not seen. I'm rereading journalism professor Dennis Covington's *Salvation on Sand Mountain,* an excellent exegesis of the author's sojourn amongst fundamentalist Christians in Alabama who pick up venomous snakes and drink poison because they believe that their faith in the Bible will preserve them. Covington is pretty clear about what draws him to these people, after he's assigned to cover the murder trial of one of their pastors. He's clear-eyed about the allure of danger and nonrational experience. Covington moves from scoffing, to fascination, to finally immersion in their world (spoiler alert!), taking up serpents himself at the climax of the book, as he takes on the indwelling of the Holy Spirit.

This is the kind of nonrationality I can understand, or at least admire, even if I can't fully enter into it as Covington could. Reading *Salvation on Sand Mountain* in the time of Covid, thinking about these old-school Appalachian faith healers and snake handlers who are confident their biblical faith will counteract venom makes me feel almost nostalgic, as though these enchanted beliefs are quaint relics of a time when everybody believed in something, even if the something didn't make a lot of sense to someone from Science World. The anarchic Denial World of the pandemic is nothing like this.

I think the proper word for Denial World is nihilism. Until now, I've associated that concept with individual pathologies, from bomb-throwing Russian anarchists to addicts in the very late stages of their compulsions, or as a pose struck by disaffected youth at various times. I've never encountered it as a collective phenomenon, unfolding in real time in front of me (more accurately, on a screen in front of me). Is this what happens when nations or civilizations are under mortal threat from an implacable antagonist, like the virus? Perhaps if I knew more about the final days of other empires, from the Sassanid to the Soviet, I might understand better. Denial World may be stored somewhere in our (meta-phorical) DNA, a psychic cartography that becomes real only under particular awful circumstances.

Why I Can't Think

I like to read pop neuroscience and so I'm familiar with the idea that during prolonged stressors such as the Covid pandemic, our survival-wiring gets jacked up and hyperactive, and bypasses the front part of our brain, where abstract thought and concentration reside. This is why I can't seem to get high-level cognitive work done—either I can't remember the word for that thing that I want to say about that other idea I don't really understand, or the facts that I'm trying to put into an order in which I can teach them to somebody sometime later keep escaping and slithering around like blobs of mercury while I stab at them vainly with my pipette.

I have read good counsel of the self-care sort that tells me to take it easy on myself, which reminds me that during a global crisis mental acuity is not likely to be optimized, and points out that uncertainty and worrying is a form of work in itself, so if I'm too tired to think straight, well, that is normal.

There's the pandemic itself, and not knowing what's going to happen tomorrow or next week, there's the tension of holding that knowledge along with the knowledge that I really am quite well off, given that I'm healthy and haven't lost my job, and there's the attachment-relationship fallout from the pandemic, including the sandwich effect of, on one hand, aging parents in precipitous mental and physical declines on the other side of the country, and on the other, the parenting stresses of sending a child back into a school system whose impending crash-and-burn is written in blazingly huge script on the calendar for September. All of this adds up to "lower your expectations of getting any work done."

Lowering my expectations is harder to do than I thought it would be. This is not what I would have predicted—I've never been a perfectionist and I believe that in almost all cases, done beats perfect. Plenty of my work is just good enough. Lowering expectations is painful not because I hold myself to inhumanly perfect standards. It's painful because letting go of academic work during a prolonged emergency means letting go of my own legend about myself.

One of the self-serving Stories of Me that forms part of my conceptual treasure hoard is about a time in grad school when I had received a research fellowship and was on my way to New York, along with other awardees from across the country, for a sort of ceremonial convocation over which a living legend in the social sciences was going to preside and dole out wisdom. It's probably notable that I can't remember now who that eminence was, although it might have been James C. Scott.

Five of us were based west of Chicago and were travelling en bloc. It was winter, and we got stuck at Chicago-Midway during a snowstorm, as the last scheduled flight of the evening into LaGuardia was cancelled. The Story of Me part is that while three of my travelling companions fussed, fretted, and pitched a hissy as only overprivileged Americans can do, I and the fifth traveller, both of us having spent years in Africa where travel was often unpredictable, found electric sockets near the floor, plonked ourselves down and plugged in our 1990s-era ThinkPads to edit our presentations. Inshallah there might be another plane that night—if not, fussing about missing the academic eminence wasn't going to accomplish anything, and we had power, heat and running water. And we could work on our ideas.

The point of that story is that I like to think of myself as the sort of person who can always get something done, adversity or no. And by "get something done," I mean "manipulate symbols and concepts in the way that has brought me the measure of professional success I now enjoy." I imagine myself as the Shetland pony of the social sciences, plodding forward through storms of personal and public life, in contrast to the high-strung Lipizzaners, which perform arabesques of scholarship only when the ring is set up just so. Some people like to go out dancing, as Lou Reed observed, and other people like us, baby, we go to work. It's a perfectly fine self-concept, until it stops functioning.

That's what I'm experiencing now, thanks to the weathering effect of the pandemic. For the first time I feel as though marshalling my ideas for writing is too hard (and I know that I'm putting the lie to this by virtue of the fact that you're reading what I will have written by the time you read it, but I think you know what I mean). Giving up on getting things done means not just adapting to an extraordinary cognitive load, it means giving up on a version of myself I've clung to, vanitas vanitatum, for twenty-plus years.

Picture a stack of papers, typescript, the sort of thing that's been rendered obsolete by screens. Now the top sheet on that stack is blowing away. Now the sheet underneath it, and now the next one. Time is passing and the pile is disassembling, dissolving into confetti. Now picture me, trying to gather up the papers, reaching out for one to restack it on the pile while another two or three drift off. That's the way my mind is working, or not working, these days, and I don't like it at all.

Fall 2020

Medicine

I took my walk today along the south side of the river, going west from the Riverside Golf Club parking lot towards Cloverdale, just below Forest Heights. It's remained a less-travelled part of the river valley, impossible to build on because of the pitch and instability of the land that drops down to the river, laced and knotted by the exposed roots of tall spruce and a few spindly poplars in the spruce shade. Getting into the area is a bit of a scramble—it angles down steeply, and the paths are not well-marked or maintained. I had to slither through a chain-link fence with a torn corner at the back of the parking lot to get in there, and I am not entirely sure that was legal.

On the other side of the fence, trails thread the forest. I encountered two men coming towards me. They were wearing baseball caps and camo jackets and paper masks, and looked to be in late middle age, by which I mean "older than me." They were both carrying double fistfuls of leafy green plants with the roots dangling, shedding dirt as they walked. I'm not always happy to run into men when I'm on my own in the less travelled parts of the river valley, but these two were laughing and joking with each other and seemed in high spirits, which put me at ease.

One man waved and asked how my day was going; I responded that it was going fine, and returned the question. "It's going great," he said. Gesturing back at the trees from which they had emerged: "This whole hill is full of medicine." He held up the plants. "These are the best medicine for your head. If my head is bothering me, I just make tea out of these and drink it." I was pretty sure he meant an actual, corporeal head, not a veiled reference to psychoactive vegetation. I said that that was really interesting, that I hadn't known there was medicine in the valley. "Full of medicine," he repeated, and the two men wished me a good day and walked off.

I didn't think much of it until a couple of weeks later when I was listening to a local-history podcast while making dinner. Podcasts are another pandemic addition to my life, because they give me human background voices, like audio wallpaper. The host was recounting a conversation with an Indigenous knowledge-keeper in the Cree tradition. According to this elder, before the settlers arrived, the amiskwaciwâskahikan area I know as Edmonton was a place of convergence for kinship groups and nations from a radius of several hundred kilometres. It was also one of the stopping points along the Old North Trail, a path made by people walking and dogs pulling travois hundreds of years ago, connecting northern Alberta with the unfathomably distant reaches of what is now Mexico.

The draw of amiskwaciwâskahikan, or Beaver Hills, was threefold: there was a broad flat area on a height commanding a view of the river, where a temporary lodge could be set up in which disputes could be settled and matters of shared governance could be discussed (not coincidentally, this is where the white settlers decided to put their provincial capitol building); there was a lot of game on the north side of the river, lending the site its name; and the south side of the river was lush with healing plants, which were most prolific in the fall, and could be picked and dried for use during the winter.

The men I met on the trail below Forest Heights were bringing medicine out of this valley, bringing a way of healing much older than the city. The plants they gathered were here long before Edmonton was. They were growing even before this place was amiskwaciwâskahikan, and will probably still be growing, leafing out and dying back, year after year, long after the Covid pandemic turns into something that happened a long time ago. The medicine of this place, the medicine that is the place, has a solidity and permanence. It has lasted throughout human habitation and it will probably outlast us too.

Masks

On Thursday I saw three instances of mask madness or the centre not holding or what you will.

The first happened at the top of the Bonnie Doon traffic circle. A man on a bike was stopped at the lights, yelling, "I'm fucking tired of you! You can't fucking do this!" At first I thought this was bike-vs-car incident escalating; then I realized he was yelling at the world in general and he was yelling about masks. "I'm tired of your fucking mask! Fucking masks don't protect you! Don't fucking tell me what to do with your fucking mask!" It was odd because he didn't have the generic urban-crazy-person dingy-grey look—he was Mr. Yuppie in expensive Italian cycling gear and a bike that was probably worth more than my car. But Mr. Yuppie was clearly losing his mind.

The second was at the Idylwylde library, where I was browsing. Staff are stationed at the doors to oversee hand sanitizing and mask use on entry and to herd us towards the hold shelves or the stacks. A frazzled middle-aged woman was remonstrating with the librarian about mask use. "I'm just here to get a book, I don't really need a mask," she kept saying, "I'm just here for the books, I'll be quick." *Well, of course you're here to get a book*, I thought but did not say. *That's the function of the library*. She did not offer reasons for why she wasn't wearing a mask (many of which would have been solid); she kept repeating she was just here to get a book, as though that in itself were a reason. After a few moments she flounced off. *Good*, I thought.

The third incident was entirely my fault. This was at the Bonnie Doon Safeway. I was walking along the cleaning products aisle and nearly bumped into an older man who glared at me and said, "Can't you read? Watch where you're going! Wear a mask and follow the arrows, it's right there in front of you!" He was right—the floors were marked with duct tape arrows indicating flow of shoppers, and I was going counter-arrow.

That night I had a very vivid dream in which there was an app on my phone that told me whether I had been in close proximity to someone with Covid. In the dream, the app was flashing red and telling me I had had six exposures in the past day. But no matter how frantically I poked at it, as my tapping of buttons escalated to whacking, it would not tell me where or how or why I had been so close to the virus, yet did not know it.

The Places Where People Are Not

In month six of the pandemic, I find myself pulled to nature—trees, ravines, shrubs, wildflowers and grasses. The less I see signs of people, the better. I don't need to go very far from buildings and streets and cars, I just need to be out of sight and hearing of them, for even a short time. I've never felt the pull this strongly before.

I've always liked being outside, but Nature with a capital N, as some sort of hallowed abstraction, is something I've always been cynical about. I've never bought into the idea of the natural world as romantic or idyllic. My earliest revolt against sentiment had to do with Nature, in the form of the treacly panentheism on offer in liberal Sunday schools, where we had to sing about "All Things Bright and Beautiful." I appreciate that this is a beloved hymn for many people, but as a child I thought that if God made the rainbows, the sunset and each little bird that sings, surely he also made the typhoon, the hornet, and the tuberculosis bacillus, which we weren't singing about. And of course, the novel coronavirus.

As I got older, I developed a more nuanced appreciation of the wild world because to me, trees and mountains and creeks meant The Places Where Other People Are Not. I have an enduring fascination with fire lookouts who spend months atop towers in the forest, or Old Believer hermits who live up Siberian rivers for decades without human contact, because I not-so-secretly want to be one myself. This has more to do with introversion than with the appreciation of the sublime.

However, I do not live in a watchtower or up a Siberian river, I live in a mid-sized city, which Covid has painted with anxiety and a subsonic hum of dread. In this pandemic city, I feel a positive compulsion to be among the trees and rivers. I'm fortunate that Edmonton has eighteen thousand acres of green space, most of it undomesticated by condos or recreational facilities, adjoining one river and three creeks. It's mainly aspen parkland, brushy and brambly, not as stark as the southern Alberta badlands or as majestic as the Rockies or as lush as the Great Lakes and St. Lawrence valley landscapes that I've lived with.

I want to *get in there*, to walk into the bush and ravine. I want to be somewhere that I can believe is untouched by human interference, and this is a desire that has come into being with the pandemic.

I know that pandemics are part of nature. We talk about the natural course of a disease or an epidemic, or about nature having its way when someone dies from Covid. But there has never been anything natural about any pandemic. If I've learned anything from studying public health, it's that all forms of generalized sickness are unnatural disasters, and the only entities who carry out this violence even though they could have done otherwise are people.

We—some of us—made the choices that caused the virus to leap across the world; we made the choices that led to, as I write, at least thirty million cases and at least a million deaths. We didn't lock down, we kept breathing on each other, we abandoned public health infrastructure that could test and trace, and we generally made this happen. And by "we" I mean mostly the powerful people in the United States, the engine of the pandemic, although not only those people, as I can see from just driving down Edmonton's main drag of bars and nightclubs, just a few blocks from home, full of unmasked people exhaling randomly for entertainment. We chose to open those bars before we opened the schools, and we chose not to provide sick leave for people who are taking care of Covid patients. We screwed this up. When I started writing these notes about Covid, I couldn't have imagined a million people dead, but that's the line the world is about to cross after six months.

When I'm around trees and rocks, the human-made world and its catastrophes recedes. It's not that I've entered an innocent Edenic space, it's more that I look around and nothing around me is culpable. I see a stand of red osier dogwood and a burst of yellow tansy and Canada geese and a coyote and the Blackmud Creek at high volume, and I see beings that are not implicated in this disaster. I am somewhere that wasn't made by people and after listening to the nightly pandemic update on the evening news, somewhere not made by people is where I want to be. (As a sociologist, I know that parks are made by people and that the decision to not build condos or strip malls in the river valley was a human one—but I'm talking about the affective experience of walking around the river valley, not the political economy).

With the arrival of fall, things are changing. Plants are dying back or taking on a final burst of colour before folding in on themselves for winter, and many of the animals are starting to leave or go to ground. Many will be gone forever. Unlike them, I will keep coming back to the ravine, with an urgency I didn't feel six months ago. I want to be somewhere that is living and dying and still guiltless. Mortal and beautiful.

Emergencies and Disasters

It's been more than half a year since the first lockdown, and when you start measuring time in years, or even parts of years, it's hard to maintain the belief that this is a crisis, an emergency, an episode, anything of short duration.

I'm reminded of people who work in humanitarian NGOs whom I've interviewed who were much concerned about the distinction between an emergency or a disaster and a...really bad never-ending situation. At the time, I thought they were being overly pedantic. If a mudslide has buried a village, does it really matter if it happened yesterday and is therefore an emergency, or six months ago and villagers still haven't been able to dig out their homes and belongings because of corruption, unpredictable storms and contaminated water, and therefore it's a complex mess with political and ecological and social dimensions? Either way, nobody has a house with an intact roof and everybody's livestock is dead.

Now I'm beginning to understand the difference between the emergency, in which you're thinking about the possibility (or impossibility) or a return to normal, and the long-term bad thing, when normal has left the building and there's just blankness where the future used to be. Right now, it looks like the world is circulating through a rise and fall and rise and fall of lockdowns, relaxations, spikes, quarantines, flattenings, parabolas, lockdowns again, ad infinitum. I am not seeing a linear path leading out of this.

In the Airport in October

I'm in transit through Pearson Airport in Toronto—first trip by air since March 13. My mother has just moved to an assisted-living residence and my father is in the hospital. I have seized the opportunity of a brief lull in case counts to go from Edmonton to Hamilton to see them, knowing that this may be the end (and indeed, from the vantage point of his death in December 2020, this will be the last time I ever see my father alive).

I have never seen an airport with so few people in motion. I had time on my hands before my Edmonton flight left, so I walked around Terminal 1 (domestic) and Terminal 3 (international). Domestic traffic looked to be down about ninety per cent from what I remember as normal, and international travel looked like it was down about eighty per cent. The only line I saw was a pinch-point funnelling people towards the international check-in desks, controlled by two security staff with temperature guns. There were many fewer bodies than normal, but the airport didn't feel depopulated. The empty spaces were filled up by the intangible and invisible knowledge of why they were empty—there's a virus out there, everybody who can stay home is doing so, and why aren't you?

I was excruciatingly aware of other travellers, far out of proportion to their numbers. My internal vigilance, always high in liminal transit spaces, was ratcheted up by the proliferation of face coverings, shields, visors, respirators and gloves, by the warning signs spelling out what two metres physical distance looked like, and by the black-masked security guards checking boarding passes to ensure that only those whose flights were leaving in the next twenty-four hours could enter the terminal.

Covid hung in the air like a miasma. Anybody might be infected. I would not have been surprised had other travellers begun glowing green or emitting a faint sulphurous odor. My consciousness of these few scattered other bodies in the airport was such that when I boarded the inter-terminal train to go to my hotel, and realized that there was no one else in the compartment, the shock and relief of being truly *alone* was far deeper than the transition from lightly-populated to unpopulated space in normal times would have warranted.

Peak Personal Responsibility

The provincial government has taken to holding live press conferences every day with the latest Covid numbers for Alberta, and I've taken to listening to them. Partly this is because I have a professional commitment to public health and so I feel like I need to know what's happening; partly this is because I'm looking for signs and omens, portents of what is coming down the road and what we can do to prevent the worst of the possible futures. I have long since concluded that the provincial government does not actually know much more than I do about the future, but the habit of hanging on the words of the chief medical officer of health persists.

Lately I'm hearing a lot about changing our ways. Smarten up, make better choices, take personal responsibility—it's not clear whether these are moral injunctions or technical advice or just empty rhetoric, gesturing to the sovereign power of the individual to make good things happen. This story about the importance of the individual, about societies comprised of individuals whose choices make everything happen, is one of the favourite stories of the Alberta government.

On one level, it's true. If everyone made the choice to not breathe on anyone else, at all, anywhere, for the next couple of months, we would be out of this. On another level, it's not true at all, because that "if everyone..." never happens. Reminding people to be responsible and make good decisions has a terrible track record in fixing public health problems. That's not what turned things around for childhood illnesses or drunk driving or smoking, and it's not going to turn things around for an infectious respiratory disease either. "Personal responsibility" is sounding more and more like a talisman and less and less like a reasoned response to Covid.

I have a growing sense of foreboding—the days are getting darker as we slide towards the winter solstice, and the future is getting darker too. Invoking the power of the individual is not even a candle-flame against the darkness anymore. So I wrote a letter to the premier and the minister of health of the United Conservative Party, the governing party in Alberta, and the chief medical officer of health. I try not to get emotional in professional correspondence, but it crept in anyway. I received no response from the officials, but I did get nearly a thousand likes and retweets on Twitter, which means...something?

Dear Premier Kenny, Minister Shandro and Dr Hinshaw,

I am a sociologist who has studied infectious disease pandemics. This is what I see in Alberta.

I think we have reached peak personal responsibility. By that I mean that after eight months of the coronavirus, everyone who is willing and able to adopt measures that will slow down transmission—wear a mask, maintain two metres distance, reduce indoor activities, stay home if sick, test—has already done so. I don't think there are gains to be made in terms of behaviour change by telling the general public to smarten up and listen to advice. That was helpful early in the pandemic, but we are past the point of diminishing returns.

We are left with people who are able to take protective measures but don't because they don't feel like it, and people who might be willing to take these measures but don't because they have reasonable grounds to fear that they would face negative consequences if they did. These consequences are mainly financial in nature—losing hours or days of work, losing one's job, losing one's business if self-employed. I have a lot more sympathy for the second group than for the first.

If nothing is done to change the decision-making environments of these groups, one of two things will happen before a vaccine arrives. The virus might decide to behave like a completely different virus and stop infecting people, cases will go down and everything will be good. Or the virus will continue to do what it does, and cases will climb until we have a full-on catastrophe. The second scenario is more likely.

I have colleagues in public health in the US. I think it's helpful to look at what is happening in American cities which are similar to Edmonton and Calgary in terms of population size and density, which are slightly ahead of us on the infection curve, and whose public health strategies have relied on reminding people to follow guidelines. I suggest you check out Columbus (Ohio), Phoenix (Arizona), Indianapolis (Indiana), and El Paso and Fort Worth (Texas), to start. Their outcomes speak for themselves so I won't go into them. They are nearing collapse of their medical systems. A few weeks ago they were where we are now. At the moment, there is nothing preventing Edmonton or Calgary from becoming like Fort Worth.

To avert this future, (some) people's behaviour needs to change. The majority of Albertans are already masking, practising social distancing and staying home when sick, but there is a minority that is not, either because they can't or because they don't want to. This requires two types of strategies, neither of which involve reminding us about personal responsibility.

The first type is aimed at people who are able to follow recommendations but don't feel like it. This means removing their opportunities to not feel like following guidelines and to thereby infect other people—closing casinos, bars, gyms, most retail, places of worship, and restaurants, checking up on people who should be isolating—and providing strong disincentives for noncompliance, in the form of curfews, fines and charges if needed.

The second type is aimed at people who might be willing to comply but can't because they fear negative consequences. This means providing rapid financial support to people who lose income because they are quarantining, are symptomatic, or are caring for sick people. It also means providing payroll support to businesses so they can continue paying employees even if the business has to close temporarily, and rent or mortgage relief paid directly to commercial tenants so they can close or reduce their activities without losing their businesses.

Some activities are essential and have to continue no matter what. Education, health, and social supports for people at greatest risk are among these, but shopping, entertaining, going to bars, and eating out are not.

I know the evidence is mixed about the effectiveness of the "hard reset," in which everything comes to a halt, as France is doing, versus the targeted lockdown in which activities are restricted in specific neighbourhoods, as New York is doing. Maybe they both work. But neither of these measures relies on recommendations and advice to the public. What was effective in the early days of the pandemic in Alberta is not going to move the needle any further after eight months.

I look forward to hearing your response to these concerns.

Resignation and the Second Wave

It's getting even darker. It's late autumn 2020, and it looks like we're going to have a second wave, or are already in one. And it looks like

Edmonton might be locked down tight again. I hoped this wouldn't happen, but it is happening.

I have options for how I respond to the fact that we're heading back into the tunnel, but not one of them is an option that I like. I can deny, refuse, and pretend it's not happening, which puts me in the same camp as the virus-deniers and anti-realists who created the second wave, which is not a camp I want to be in. I can rail impotently against the amorphous public that did not social-distance, stay home when sick, or get tested, but that does nothing for the amorphous public while it corrodes me with toxic frustration. Or I can resign myself.

Sometimes when I'm thinking about something I don't want to think about, like another six months spent in the isolation and anxiety of a pandemic, I start gnawing on the words that I think with, as a distraction from what the words signify. Resignation. Resigning oneself. Leaving office, putting aside a status, stepping down or stepping back. If I resign myself, it is something that I do, but also something that is done to me. I am active and passive in that sentence, which is similar to my agency in this pandemic.

I wonder about the "sign" of resignation. Online etymology tells me that it comes from the Old French "resigner," which in turn has to do with Latin and accountancy—specifically, the act of cancelling one mark in an account book with another, authorized by an individual's identifying mark or signature. In the oldest uses of the word, a credit nullifies or "resigns" a debt, an addition to the balance sheet resigns a subtraction.

Maybe I can work with this. Resigning myself to the second wave need not mean a helpless and pointless stasis. I can sign this time of trouble with my own mark, and I can resign, at least in part, the losses to Covid. I can find ways to experience life in the time of Covid as not only and always deficit and loss, but also, possibly, something on the other side of the great ledger. Resignation, in this archaic sense, might also be re-signification—endowing events and experiences with meaning. I can't change anything of this, so I might as well try to re-sign it, re-sign myself.

I need to be precise about what I mean by re-signing myself to the pandemic, in that archaic sense of resignation. I don't want to go down the icky yellow-brick road of bright-siding the pandemic, seeing opportunities for self-development and silver linings. That's the road of extreme individualism, built on the presumption of affluence and free time for leisurely contemplation, insulated from the possibility that things might get really bad. I am not insulated from that possibility—indeed, I spend a lot of time thinking about how things might get really bad. I am not finding a silver lining. I am not experiencing the pandemic as moral therapy; on the contrary, I have a first-order aversion to the condition I find myself in.

What does re-signification look like? I need to think about that for a while longer.

The River is Alive

With the second wave rising, spending time in large indoor public spaces is looking even less appealing, and they're probably going to close down soon anyway. So, back to the river valley. The more time I spend wandering around there, the more my sense of Edmonton's gravity shifts, downwards, to the North Saskatchewan and the aspen parklands around it.

Pre-Covid, I had very few thoughts about the North Saskatchewan. All the cities I've lived in have had a river or lake as one of the main orienting features, so the idea that a river runs through it is not new. Edmonton's river valley is for the most part what's called undeveloped, meaning that there aren't many buildings made by people and a lot of the trails are just dirt or gravel, so when I think about commerce, entertainment, politics, civic life—that's what happens up out of the valley, and the pull of the river is weak indeed.

Now I'm noticing in a new way that the river is alive. Literally alive—I've seen beavers and foxes and coyotes and small groups of people fishing on the sandbars and accidental beaches revealed when the water is low, so there must be something in there that people can eat. Also alive in a not so literal sense, in that I see how the river makes life happen, makes things possible, small in scale but possessing some vital spirit, that can't be seen from the heights of the valley. I've seen naked toddlers running in and out of the shallows of Mill Creek, concealed by underbrush. I've seen paddlers and kayakers putting in and taking out at the foot of 50th Street. I've seen the broken trails down through the shrubs made by dogs plunging into the water from the off-leash areas. I haven't seen anyone fully immersed and swimming, because this river is fed by glacial meltwater, but I've seen people partway in the water, dropping sticks in the water to see if they float, and using the water to move a little further down the banks from where they were. I remember hearing from an Indigenous professor that the name "Saskatchewan" means "the river that moves at the speed of a person walking," and I've adapted my own pace to the current. The river has become human-scale in a way that it wasn't when I knew it mainly as a wavy line on a map.

This return to the human scale of the river feels like a return to a history that I was never part of. For millennia, and for centuries and for decades, within the memory of people alive today, the river was saturated with commerce and transportation. For thousands of years, it was the main way to get from the Rocky Mountains to the eastern prairie. When people travelled by land rather than water, their trails paralleled the river.

When white people started arriving in the 19th century, living on the river (or controlling land next to the river and booting out the people who were already living there) was a political and economic preoccupation of the settler governments, particularly of Frank Oliver, the xenophobic expansionist mayor of early twentieth-century Edmonton. In the mid-twentieth century, Mill Creek was a centre of small-scale and precarious industrial activity: a pottery, a brewery, a slaughterhouse—all now abandoned with only the odd building foundation remaining. There was a small grinding mill at the outflow of the creek for a few years in the late 1890s.

I'm reminded of Sarah Moss's description of the North Atlantic islands—the Hebrides, the Faroes, Scilly, Aran. Their waterscapes are much more dramatic than mine, especially since the surge of the North Saskatchewan was tamed by the Brazeau Dam in the 1960s. Nonetheless, what Moss says about the water and the land rings true. She points out that twenty-first-century north Europeans tend to think of the North Atlantic as wild, perhaps scenic, but remote. Commerce and civic life happens inland with the road system connecting towns and transporting people and goods; the water is "out there." But a thousand years ago, the North Atlantic coast was the "sea road." These waterways were well-travelled as people moved along them to go north and west and return. The hinterland, the place where people didn't come and go, was the inland.

The sea road makes me think of Edmonton's River Valley Road. It's a place name for a drive connecting the western part of downtown to the southeastern side of the city, which runs parallel to the North Saskatchewan for most of the way. It's a road that happens to be next to a river, not a river that is a road. But when I'm down in the river valley, out of my car, next to the water, I can feel the weight of the river and the pull of people walking, playing, moving in and out of the water. My psychogeographical gravity has shifted, and the river is no longer a periphery but a living thing.

De-Escalation

I'm perturbed by the weird lake of anger that is simmering just below the surface of only mildly frustrating everyday interactions. My threshold for annoyance, irritation, disquiet has been pushed way down by Covid, because the pandemic keeps the alarm circuitry taut and quivering—it doesn't take much to pluck it. It is possible that anger is substituting for anxiety.

Fortunately or not, I come from a cultural background better known for repressing any expression of emotion than for putting it all out there, so I haven't said or done (too many) things that I regret. But I've wanted to. The self that wants to yell or ruminate furiously and the self that knows that neither of these responses to minor stressors is a good idea are coexisting uneasily.

The result is a sort of Covid-induced ego-dystonia, in which I feel distress about the distance between these selves. Who is this person who is wildly reactive to small triggers? I'm the person who keeps calm and carries on, the person who draws down the bad energy of situations gone sideways. I am not the person who pumps them up or who fantasizes about actions, such as yelling or slamming things around, which if I were to put them into play would make the situation much worse. Except maybe I am that person, during Covid.

A couple of weeks ago I was in a store. A woman with no mask was making the rounds of browsing customers, asking for money. She didn't look entirely well, with a combination of too-bright eyes and a greyish assortment of clothes. Because she was maskless, I registered her facial expression strongly. Another shopper took exception to the requests for money and told the woman to get out: "You're putting us in danger, you're breaking the law." The maskless woman was not about to be told what to do and moved quickly towards the back reaches of the store. The intervenor followed her, cellphone out and recording. Voices were raised. One person shoved another, the other person shoved back, and both were soon yelling at the store clerk to call the police: "She won't wear her mask and she assaulted me!" and "I have a right not to mask and I'm disabled, and she hit me!" The clerk yelled back that they both had to leave the store. Neither one was about to concede that ground.

I could feel conflict de-escalation balls falling into place in my brain, like a pinball game just before the player releases the lever. I went over to the masked complainer, who appeared the most amenable to de-escalation, and murmured about empathy and distraction. "I know, it's so frustrating, I totally get how you're feeling, these are stressful times, you probably just want to shop in peace," et cetera, et cetera, while the store manager and the security guard conferred over what to do. After what was probably only a minute or so, the maskless woman headed for the exit of her own accord, announcing that she wouldn't come back and her human rights had been violated. The intervenor sighed enormously and started texting her friends with the video of the encounter. Incident over.

I was relieved, not just because I'd managed to avoid witness-ing more unpleasantness, but because I had managed to go towards the problem and dial it down, at least a little bit. I was not the one who ranted or panicked. I tried to do something helpful, even if I didn't know that it actually helped. I can still attempt to embody the Good Citizen, even if she has to share psychic space with the Angry Other. I am still recognizable to myself, at least some of the time.

Normalized/Panicked

How many forms can cognitive dissonance take? I keep discovering more, like opening a pandemic Pandora's box.

Today's special is normalized/panicked. Our case numbers are ten times what they were in April, test positivity is over four per cent, hospitals are cancelling elective procedures, yet seen from the angle of mundane life it's all just a bit tedious but unremarkable. Here's another Covid letter from the school board, my kid's school is officially in out-break—looks like it's just the grade eights who have to quarantine, no big deal. I should really take my laptop in to get fixed now. Looks like we're heading for another shutdown and the Apple store might be closed. The library will probably be one of the first places to go so I'd better put on hold those books that I want to read. Covid-adjustment has become as anodyne as the air I breathe, which is an unfortunate metaphor.

Zoom out to a wider angle, to the province and the country and the world, and the atmosphere gets thicker, darker and smokier. This is the realm of the almost constant freak-out. It cannot possibly get any worse. It cannot—it just did. This can't be real. Yes it is real. Is there an end? Will there ever be a time after? How many people are going to die? What's going to happen to the hospitals? Am I living through the collapse of western society? France is locked down again—the whole country! This is the sensation of plunging, of tipping over backward with no sense of the ground below.

My conscious self is sliding back and forth constantly between these modes, like a bead on a string. In normal mode, the panicked side looks extreme and a bit silly. In panicked mode, the routinized dailiness of normalization looks like dangerous denial. I don't think there's a centre point, an equilibrium from which I can thoughtfully consider the value of each perspective. Perhaps this is because they don't feel like two perspectives, they feel like two realities, which can't coexist, yet must coexist.

It's All Fucking Bullshit

Yesterday waiting in line at the Apple store to get my laptop serviced, a man several spots ahead of me got upset because the wait was up to forty-five minutes to see a tech support person for whatever issue his phone was having.

He told the Apple staffer whose job was to manage the queue that this was fucking bullshit. Then he told the security guard who came over to cool him down that this was fucking bullshit. Then in case anyone in the queue had missed his point, he turned around and glared at the rest of us and announced that it was all fucking bullshit. Then he stalked out of the queue and the mall, talking loudly on his phone, telling his invisible friend that it was, yes, fucking bullshit.

This afternoon, I was on a long walk with a friend. It was one of those fall days that's a throwback to summer—golden haze in the air, the only sign of impending winter the patchworks of beige and caramel and wheat colours where green used to be. We were crossing the bridge on the home-stretch of the walk and encountered a woman walking towards us from the other end of the bridge, with the bent-forward, arms-pumping gait that signifies a bad day. "You don't have to hog the whole fucking bridge," she hissed at us as she passed.

We were not hogging the whole fucking bridge. The wooden pedestrian walkway was at least two metres wide, and my friend and I were walking side by side, with only easy conversation distance between us. We displaced this woman's furious trajectory by at most a quick shuffle to the left.

These displays of anger left me feeling obscurely ashamed, as an unwilling voyeur of emotional disrobing. It's as though people are wearing their insides on their outsides, fear and nervousness and dis-inhibition glistening like viscera.

Watching the Election

The US election brought on another bout of the strange crisis prox-emics of the pandemic condition. For the previous two elections, in 2016 and 2012, I'd been at watch parties in friends' houses. I was in the company of people I sort of knew but didn't really, even though I worked with most of them, and we waited for the same elevators or passed in the same hallways several times a week.

This year I was in my bedroom, which is also where I am most of the time, and the party is the rectangles on the Zoom screen. This group was a collection of friends from high school, some of whom I had not seen in any form for thirty-five years. The pandemic, which made us all bored and lonely and brought Zoom into our lives, had opened a space in which we could be drawn back to each other again, reactivat-ing very old and very dormant gravitational pulls from the time when we were in each others' lives every day, because we had to be and sometimes because we wanted to be. Getting back together to watch election returns would have been unthinkable a year ago, at least to me. The pandemic changed the distances amongst us, making it possible and even desirable to come back together. It was a good evening despite the anxious moments when Trump seemed to be pulling ahead. Lots of laughing, which is not something I do much of anymore, and benign showings-off of pets and kids.

This reconstitution of vanished social groupings is a Covid phenomenon. As the pandemic drags on, I've dropped out of contact with people I used to see on the regular, like the people who took the same elevator that I did at work, but others have come into my life, or rather have come back from earlier moments—high school, undergrad, summer camp, summer jobs, grad school, extended family, their circumstances and preoccupations and ways of being all mediated by the screen, moving from strange to recognizable to familiar again: yes, I remember, that person is like this or like that, how remarkable that we moved apart and yet here we are again. Not in the same place of physical space and geography, but also in the same place, in the same boat or in some other vehicle lurching through the pandemic.

Covid loneliness, and the drive to overcome the loneliness, has shown me my biography spread out like a map of city lights, clusters of social glow, separated by dark filaments of time like highways. I seem to be always driving out of these cities with the car radio on, losing the local stations to static, and then slowly the signals from other stations, other times, start to come in, segueing from silence into voices. This is something I have Covid to thank for: bringing me back these parts of my past.

The Fresh Horrors Device

"* Wakes up and looks at phone * Ah let's see what fresh horrors await me on the fresh horrors device," tweeted someone going by Miss O'Kistic, about their smartphone, in November 2016. Almost three years later I am eyeing my iPhone as I would an unstable isotope or a bag of meth—if I touch it, bad things are going to happen, and yet I know I'm going to touch it.

The bad thing today is knowledge of Covid counts. Sober and conservative projections are for over a quarter of a million deaths in the United States by the first week in December. Eleven million American cases to date. Fifty-four million in the world. In my corner, daily new cases in Alberta have passed the thousand-case mark and medical staff are warning that hospital care will collapse in the coming weeks. I read that Covid is growing exponentially, but I don't think I can fully grasp what "exponential growth" means. I don't know if human minds can handle the speeding-up, the acceleration beyond arithmetical increases. It's like the worst kind of time travel.

Uncharted territory, unknown waters, the abyss—geographic metaphors are pressed into service to describe something for which we have no experiential language. I literally do not know what to say about these numbers, but just as I can't stop picking up the fresh horrors device, I also can't stop talking to myself about Covid, even if I can't find the words.

Other strange things are happening. A few days ago, on the Terwillegar footbridge crossing the river, a bald eagle swooped down not three metres from me. It skimmed the handrail, swung up and around and looked at me, and then took off for a tree on the riverbank. I have never been so close to a bird of prey before. On my neighbourhood NextDoor site, the discussion forum is filling up with pictures of coyotes in the snow. They're appearing in parks and schoolyards in Ottewell and Holyrood, adjacent to the river valley, not just one at a time but in packs of up to eight. They are magnificent, and neighbours are telling each other to keep small children and pets indoors.

In another century these appearances might fall into the category of "signs and wonders" (in another century, I wouldn't know about them because there would be no internet, but that's not the point). Even a year ago, unexpected predators in new territory might have seemed ominous. Today it is oddly comforting, a reminder that the universe holds more than fresh horrors. If the exponential explosions are coming from a future that's arriving much too fast, the coyotes and the eagle in their slow stalking, their graceful hunger, seem like emissaries from another world.

The Campsite

I went to the river valley to walk because staying inside my four walls today was starting to seem not quite bearable. I took the Forest Heights trail—south side of the river, just west of Dawson Bridge, leading off from the currently-almost-empty parking lot of the Riverside Golf Club on Rowland Road. This trail bends and branches into smaller trails, up and down sharp-angled approaches to the river that drop away abruptly. In the snow I saw tire tracks from what must have been a mountain bike, and imagined someone careening along these skinny switchbacks through scruffy jackpine and manitoba maple.

One mini-trail branched off and led to a point overlooking the river, about five metres above the water. The path ended beside a campsite. Someone had set up a couple of tarps strung over small trees, hung a large metal pail by the handle from a broken branch, and rigged up what looked to me like a bear bag—a sturdy plastic sack to keep food and toiletries away from bears—suspended between two spruce. I saw the blackened sticks of a small fire pit. Snow had fallen recently and had not been disturbed, and the tarps were sagging slightly under the weight. Under the new snow I could see the outlines of footprints. Someone had been here in the recent past, but not yesterday or today.

Somewhere around six hundred people are sleeping rough in Edmonton on any given night, most of them in the river valley. I've come across the remains of tents scattered across the banks and have been mindful of steering clear of the larger semi-permanent encampments in the ravine near my home. This, however, was the first time I'd encountered something that looked a lot like someone had set up a place where they planned to stay. The view over the river was magnificent—houses on the opposite bank sold for close to a million dollars—but the site was completely hidden from anyone passing on the main trail.

I thought that this spot must be very familiar to someone. Somebody must come and go from here, someone must arrive here at the end of a day or a night with the knowledge of coming home. This is someone's place. I may be romanticizing the situation. Sleeping outdoors in an Edmonton winter would frankly be terrifying, and no matter how good the view, whoever was living here would probably be much better off somewhere with four stable walls and central heating.

Still, I wondered who that person was, and where they were. Why hadn't they come back since the recent early snowfall? Were they in search of food, did they have their supplies in the makeshift bear bag, did they melt snow or ice for water over the fire pit? I did not want to meet that person, and I did not want to trespass on their domain. I turned around and clambered back to the main trail. I imagined this person, like me, just getting through the days.

Pandemic Melancholy

The second wave is here, and Alberta is the epicentre for Canada, and there's no sign that our leaders are willing to make the decisions that will get us out of it, which is all I'll say about politics for now.

I had my first experience of Covid nostalgia today, or maybe it was melancholy. I had to pick up a parcel from FedEx, and the parcel depot is located a few blocks from the cheer gym my daughter used to attend (I notice that I wrote "used to attend," rather than "attends", but I will leave this sentence as-is). It's a major road so I pass the gym a lot en route to one thing or another.

The sight of the lime-green logo always trips a little memory-wire in my mind, and I associate the place with good times, with feeling

pride in my daughter's accomplishments and enjoyment in the spec-
tacles her team pulled together. I also associate it with tedium, waiting
around after practice, awkward small talk with other moms perching
in the cabs of giant blocky SUVs, and feeling twinges of annoyance
that I spend so much of my very limited time driving around the suburbs with my phone wedged beside the stick shift, trying to decipher
Google Maps directions to competitions held in giant underventilated
sportsplexes.

The pandemic, however, has turned down the volume on the
boring memories and turned up the volume on the anticipatory, aspira-
tional and exciting ones. These memories cast a light forward into the
unknown future of the pandemic—when this is all over, or at least different, we'll get back to the gym, cheer will restart as it should be, and
that will be a happy day. The gym has served as a sort of touchstone
for past and future, the way things were and the way I expect them
to be again.

It felt different today. I experienced a sharper trip on the psychic
wire, a sadness for not only what had happened in the past but for
what would not happen in the future. Memories were triggered, but in
an odd doubled way (as almost everything now is both odd and doubled). I remembered last year, the good times that were great times
and the good times that were merely ordinary boring times, but I also
remembered the hope and the misplaced confidence I had invested in
the gym more recently.

Two months ago, I was thinking in terms of "when we go back…";
today I'm not. Two months ago, I imagined a future I'm not able to
imagine today. I don't see a way out of this pandemic, and I don't see a
way into next year. Passing the empty parking lot as I turn left into the
light industrial area with the long quiet warehouses, I'm in a small way
grieving not only the past, but also the past of the future. The future
isn't what it used to be, in the first few months of the pandemic.

I have no background in psychoanalysis, but I read Freud's
"Mourning and Melancholia" a few years ago, and I believe that what
I'm experiencing is closer to melancholia than grief or nostalgia. That

imagined day in 2021 when all the kids and all the moms go back to cheer was never real. It was always contingent, always fantastical. I am sad because of the loss of something that never existed except as an impossibility.

When I got home, I searched for a YouTube video that was circulating sometime last summer. It's shot inside American hospitals, during the worst of the spring Covid surge. Nurses and physicians began a ritual of calling "Code Rocky" for Covid patients when they were discharged. The theme from *Rocky* blares out from speakers as departing patients are wheeled triumphantly by caregivers through a crowd of waving, cheering health care workers. It's utterly clichéd and utterly charming.

Watching it now, six months later, I still feel the frisson of hope and excitement. Music never disappoints, even the most overdone. But I also remember how I used to feel when I played it over and over half a year ago. I was imagining a future filled with Code Rockys, triumphant returns and re-inhabitations of places and gatherings and connections, a future which now appears to have never really existed at all.

Winter 2021

Time of Trial

When the first heavy snow fell and winter started closing in, I started to wonder what the loneliness and isolation would be like during the dark months ahead. I recognized that it's really not good to be at home without other adults and working all the time, especially because "all the time" feels quite different in month eight than it did in month one or two. I know I'm lucky that I have work that can be done at home, and that there's no foreseeable change in my salary. I have the luxury of contemplating what enforced solitude will be like, because I don't have to contemplate instead where the mortgage money is going to come from.

Moving into winter this year feels like plunging into a tunnel, or being engulfed by a tunnel that comes up strong and fast. I'm preparing for a solitary time of trial, fitted out with winter gear scavenged from Goodwill and Value Village, because this has to be the year that I finally get past my horror of being cold. For the past twenty years, I've fostered the conceit that I can never really get warm in Edmonton in the winter, that I have to stay homebound most of the time because there's no way I can tolerate thirty degrees below zero. Time to get rid of that conceit this year. Time to do battle with the cold.

An absurd image floats into my mind from a childhood book about medieval Europe and chivalry, of knights preparing themselves for combat with midnight vigils of contemplation in the chapel, followed by armour and weapons chosen the next day. On second thought, perhaps not so absurd, given that I've started referring to Covid as "the plague" or "the pestilence," my attempt at sardonic irony that's also redolent of antiquity.

Once winter really sets in, I don't want screens and social media to become my lifeline to the outside world, yet I fear that's going to happen. These technologies are bare threads, all the texture stripped away. The ties that connect during normal times weave in and out, braided and coiled ropes like the ones that hold dinghies to the dock, or connect fishing boats rolling on the waves.

The connections in Covid time, parsed out through blinking lights on little screens, do not feel like ropes at all. They have the paltry width and heft of the loops of jewellers' wire I bring back from the craft store to string beads on, all surface shine, but so frangible and easily snapped.

Vacation Scandal

I've been reading the news about the United Conservative Party and the revelations that at least six members of the provincial Legislative Assembly went off for Christmas vacations in sunny destinations like Mexico and Arizona. They left Alberta in mid-December to vacation with family and friends, at the height of the pandemic second wave, in the process contravening the federal avoid-nonessential-travel advisory, and then provided vague or implausible accounts of their whereabouts. I'm trying to not write much about politics here, but what's taking shape in my mind as I follow the tweets and news articles and online commenting isn't so much partisan-political as ethical-emotional, so here I go.

On the surface, this is just another elite entitlement scandal. The premier didn't do anything except to say that his people hadn't technically broken the law and that he was disappointed.

I can't believe I actually need to write this sentence, but hypocrisy and deception are not good looks on a government, and so for that reason alone this is really bad. But the timing of this particular scandal makes it much worse.

We are eight (nine?) months into the pandemic. For the first few weeks, it was an emergency. But it wasn't a dystopian horror. Despite a genre of cultural myths about the Lord of the Flies and every-man-for-himself chaos, as a sociologist I know that when emergencies strike, people usually want to help each other. One of the foundational books in disaster sociology is Rebecca Solnit's *A Paradise Built In Hell*, in which she details acts of solidarity, mutual support and compassion in the wake of wildfires, earthquakes and terrorist attacks. I don't know if this is human evolutionary brain wiring or cultural conditioning kept alive through moral and ethical teachings, but when disasters strike, most people want to do something good.

On a global level, the pandemic produced an upward bounce for public trust in government institutions in almost all wealthy countries, as measured by opinion surveys (the exception is the United States, which is an entirely different story). The conventional wisdom in socio-logical studies of public trust in government is that it's been declining over the last few decades, but crises like terrorist attacks or plague outbreaks boost it back up—many of us believe, or want to believe, that elite leaders are trying to prevent deaths or disasters. In Canada, the big exception to the trust bounce are Indigenous peoples, who have good reason to believe that governments don't really care if they live or die, and who can plausibly say to the non-Indigenous population: you should have seen this coming.

In the first few weeks of the pandemic, I saw good things in Alberta. Edmonton and Calgary stopped charging bus fares. Sikh orga-nizations set up free grab-and-go meals for truckers. Entire neighbour-hoods cheered for medical workers every night at seven. Little Free Libraries proliferated. Mutual-help networks sprang up. In my neigh-bourhood, the community league's impromptu help-your-neighbour clearinghouse got bogged down by everyone who wanted to help with the requests that were coming in ("Senior couple in Kenilworth needs prescriptions picked up, who can do it?," "I got this one!," "I got it too!," "Okay, next one is mine!" and so forth). There were hoarders and creeps, but there was also goodwill and desire to bring this pandemic to an end. #WereAllInThisTogether was a hashtag, but also a way of being. I felt almost warm and sentimental about #FlatttenTheCurve and #MyMaskProtectsYou, even as I fussed about where to get respi-rators and whether I had enough isopropyl alcohol.

It didn't last. After nine months, collective ebullience and resilience are running on empty. The pandemic has been worse than anyone other than an epidemiologist expected. I really did not think that I would still be isolating on New Year's Day 2021. I'm noticing that the go-this-way arrows in the grocery stores are getting worn down and I can't tell which way to go anymore, which is a metaphor for something. It's been long enough to wear vinyl stickers into illegibility.

Also, lots of people are dead—over a thousand in Alberta. That's a lot of grief and trauma, especially where these Covid deaths took place under pandemic conditions, people seizing or asphyxiating alone in overcrowded hospitals. On top of the Covid deaths came all the other deaths and sicknesses that were not directly caused by the virus but were bad because of the virus—the people who died from other causes, but also without friends or family near them, or the non-fatal but still painful physical and mental health crashes that happened because of anxiety and isolation. Grief and fear and sadness are sky-high, boiling up in everyday encounters and writ large in collective collapses. And I haven't even mentioned the economic hardships of the stuttering lockdown-open-up-mockdown-lockdown cycles that the provincial government has put us through. Alberta is not a normal population anymore. It is a traumatized population.

I'm struck by how many people view these vacations by government members through the prism of their own pain. It's not just "these people abused their privileges," it's "these people abused their privileges while I was suffering." Stories of unattended parental and grandparental deaths, friends and kin and neighbours collapsing under mental health stressors, and frontline health workers burning themselves into exhaustion are boiling just under the surface of furious condemnations of the premier and his people. I have my own story in this treasury, about the unattended death of a parent, but I'm not telling that story here.

Political corruption always breeds cynicism. However, under the prolonged trauma and fatigue that is the Covid pandemic, corruption breeds things that are worse than cynicism.

One outcome of trauma, individual or collective, is learned helplessness, the awareness that no matter what you do, the outcome won't change. Helplessness breeds apathy, and that's what this vacation mess is teaching us. I've been social-distancing and masking and sanitizing for months. My life has been thrown up in the air by the stringencies of virus control. (And I'm on the fortunate end of the disruption spectrum because I'm still employed and no one in my household has gotten sick). If I knew that my sacrifice and others' sacrifice was helping to stop Covid, I would count it worthwhile. But everything we do is getting undone. The advice we were given was never meant to be taken seriously. Our leaders clearly don't believe in it. On top of this, there's a super-contagious variant on its way from the UK. Nothing I do is going to change the pandemic. Why should I even pay attention anymore?

And especially, why should I pay attention to these jack-asses? They punked us. They played us. They created elaborate fake Christmas pictures to tweet out on social media. They think we're stupid. If these people are telling me I ought to do something to be a good citizen, I want to do the opposite, even if the opposite is self-destructive. If I listen to these people at all. If I care about this at all anymore. #StayHomeSaveLives? What a joke.

On the other side of the aisle from the virtuous-yet-punked people are the virus-deniers and the anti-vaxxers and the virus-skeptics. This anti-science worldview arises from fear, and is therefore always unstable, always in search of corroboration. And now they have some. If the virus was that bad, would all these people be vacationing abroad? The government says one thing—dangerous virus, very serious, must respect science, follow instructions, stay home—and does another. Look at what they do. They know this pandemic isn't real. They know the science is a joke. And what's this vaccine? More fakery. Do you trust what they say? Why not trust your own instincts, which will tell you what you *really* want to hear?

Seeing elites breaking the rules is insidious. It even has a name now—the (Dominic) Cummings effect, after the press secretary for UK Prime Minister Boris Johnson who went off on a well-publicized road trip around England at a time when everyone was supposed to be staying home. Political scientist Daisy Fancourt and a team of British researchers traced the rise in public cynicism about lockdown orders to Cummings's vacation tour. Seeing that my elected representative went to Hawaii does not mean I'm going to go to Hawaii, but it means going to Hawaii in the midst of the pandemic is now firmly within the realm of the thinkable and the doable.

And if going to Hawaii contra all travel advisories is doable, so are smaller transgressions like foregoing a mask, having a party in the back yard, or pressuring baristas to open up for indoor seating. Even if the better angels of my nature disapprove of this behaviour on principle, the seed of the idea that such behaviour is possible and makes life more enjoyable has been planted. Public health advisories are reconfigured into the flimsy fences and barriers of a parkour obstacle course—with a little bit of ducking and dodging, anybody can find their way around them, and why not?

It did not have to be this way. People are not hardwired to be invariably apathetic, mistrusting and fearful. If anything, the early days of the pandemic showed that there's a strong current of goodwill, of the desire to do something right. But after the better part of a year, the reservoir is drained, and in its place there's a lot of seething pain, trauma and anger. The pandemic is going to get worse because of people who went on holiday, and not because they may have spread the virus in their travels or brought back a new strain of SARS-CoV-2. Toxic cynicism and apathy can kill, especially when preying on a population that's already weakened by months of loss. The provincial leaders could have safeguarded the resilience and solidarity that was present at the beginning of the pandemic, but they chose to blow it away instead.

Schadenfreude

I am experiencing a twisted form of inverse schadenfreude, thanks to Covid. Instead of being happy about the misfortune of others, I am angry about the pleasures and enjoyments of others. Specifically, I am becoming angrier and angrier at the thought of people going about their business, living their lives blithely shopping, eating out and generally following a pre-pandemic delineation of recreation and fun.

I don't mean people who must put themselves out on the frontlines like health care workers or grocery clerks, I mean the people that I imagine inhabiting the hulking SUVs parked at the casino, or the ones that I can see through the spacious and sunny windows of the new bistro/bakery that's opened up in an old industrial space a few blocks away.

This is anger mixed with no small amount of self-righteousness. I have been diligently social-distancing, keeping the rules, sacrificing peace of mind and freedom and enjoyment—but these people (the ones who don't do all the right things that I do) are squandering my best efforts, blithely spending down the horde of caution that I've been accumulating coin by tiny coin. And so we now have a situation in which one out of forty-three people in Alberta has been diagnosed with Covid, and over five hundred are dead. I realize there's not quite a straight line between the daily death count and the café loungers, but the line doesn't have that many twists and turns in it either. It's a communicable disease—so stay home, wear a mask, don't communicate it.

I can't even console myself by thinking, "well, I'm all right— they're going to get infected and maybe get horribly sick with long Covid because they didn't take precautions, but I won't!" Realistically, I was never really in danger of becoming one of the statistics. I'm (relatively) young-ish, in ridiculously good health, and with access to excellent medical care. I haven't saved myself from death or severe debilitation, because I really wasn't in that lineup to begin with. I just followed the public health rules and did what I was told because…it made sense, and because I'm in the habit of following rules.

This reverse-schadenfreude effect becomes stronger as the possibility of a vaccine becomes more real. On that day in the mythical future when we're able to emerge back into public life, I imagine finding those people who've spent the pandemic in coffee shops and gyms and restaurants still there, relaxed and well-fed and well-provisioned, as though nothing ever happened at all. The sacrifices that so many people underwent to try to stem the tide of infections, and my sacrifice (which is nothing compared to what other people gave up) will be invisible. We won't be able to claim any rewards for special restraint, because the only reward is the return to a world in which this special restraint is not important any more.

Having these thoughts makes me feel both cranky and petty—why can't I be selfless and glad to be able to make the sacrifices? Yet knowing that I am cranky and petty doesn't stop me from being so.

Hermits

I've always had a second life in books, a steady stream of reading running parallel to my external life of work, parenting, shopping, cleaning and mundane as well as extraordinary events. Sometimes the streams cross, as off-the-page transitions and preoccupations manifest in bursts of reading. I can see this confluence more clearly in the books I borrow, rather than the ones I buy. Book-buying is investment behaviour—am I still going to want to read this in five years? Is this of sufficient quality that I want to have it around forever? Book borrowing is consumption behaviour—what do I want to know about right now? What's speaking to me in this moment, when I know the moment may not last forever?

One of the effects of the new Alberta lockdown, coming in less than 72 hours, is that city libraries will close. I've been on the library website putting books on hold and crossing my fingers that the holds get delivered to my local branch before everything goes down once again. That meant I had the opportunity to review my borrowing. Themes emerge.

Over the course of the pandemic, I borrowed a lot of books about hermits, recluses, and people who don't want to be around other people. This line ran through everything from highbrow (the journals of Thomas Merton and accounts of the Desert Fathers) to pop culture (*Stranger in the Woods: The Extraordinary Tale of the Last True Hermit*, who hid out for twenty-seven years in rural Maine, helping himself to anything that wasn't locked up in local holiday homes). I also re-read *Into the Wild*, about the death of Christopher McCandless in Alaska, in its second edition, as well as a somewhat disappointing tell-all memoir by his sister that suggests that McCandless disappeared from society because the family was dysfunctional rather than because he wanted to be away from everyone. On a rare foray into the books section of Value Village, I was very happy to find not only *Deep Survival*, a guide to what to do if you're tipped from a whitewater raft into a freezing river torrent, but also a group biography of the first women to ascend various Himalayan peaks (*Savage Summit*), often coming down with horrifying forms of altitude sickness and frostbite in the process.

My list of streaming video that I've accessed through the library contains not only the documentary version of "Stranger in the Woods," but also a series of Russian public-broadcasting documentaries about Agafia Lykova, the "loneliest woman in Russia," who has lived by herself in the Siberian backwoods for seventy years as the last of a family of Old Believers who fled into the bush after the Russian revolution, and a Great Courses lecture video about Daoist recluses in sixteenth-century China.

I also appear to be really interested in the polar regions. I've borrowed the Rough Guide to Antarctica, which has a lot of practical information, as well as *Terra Incognita: Travels in Antarctica,* which has some literary value, and a slew of travel literature and gruesome stories about the Scott and Shackleton expeditions. Most recently, I've been borrowing travel books about Greenland, the Yakutsk region of Siberia, and Baffin Island.

The connection between this parallel book-life and the life outside of books is not subtle. I'm heading into a period of semi-voluntary isolation during which I will do my best to avoid other humans, during the darkest and potentially coldest parts of the year, in a very far northern city. As with everything I experience, I want to know how other people have done it, what is possible and what is impossible, how to do this with some degree of grace or fortitude. My ideal guide would probably be a contemplative nun who built a hermitage on the Larsen Ice Shelf and after twenty years decided to hike out to McMurdo Antarctic Base, but so far that hasn't come up in the library's "Recommended for You" algorithm.

Buffalo Bill's Defunct

Last week the US Capitol was besieged. A mob of Trump supporters broke through to try to stop the certification of the vote that made Joe Biden the next president. It looked like wartime. The mob has been put down now, and I'm living through a lot of thoughts and feelings about the US. As a half-American who's profoundly alienated from the country where I was born because of its deep-down racism and violence, I am also, whether I like it or not, equally profoundly tied to it by a not entirely rational belief that it can and must become a better place. This is probably the result of my early infusion of shining-city-on-a-hill mythology (which, as an adult, I can now critique six ways from Sunday), enhanced by the quasi-religious traditions of the civil rights era and its legacy all the way down to Obama.

With the insanity at the Capitol, in addition to thinking "WTF is wrong with you people?! You have to respect the vote! You're betraying everything! You can't do that!", I had bits of a poem running through my head and now, as soon as I heard that a US president had been impeached a second time, I've figured out which one:

Buffalo Bill's
defunct
            who used to
            ride a watersmooth-silver
                                    stallion
and break onetwothreefourfive pigeonsjustlikethat
                                                    jesus

he was a handsome man
                        and what i want to know is
how do you like your blue-eyed boy
Mister Death

Be Kind

Today I was driving home from errands, listening to the local CBC afternoon programs on the radio. The hosts were wrapping up a week of call-ins and fundraising for Be Kind Week, a Covid innovation in which listeners were invited to phone in with their stories of kind deeds and to pledge money for the food bank. The fundraising goal was half a million dollars; the total raised was more than double that amount. The hosts were very happy, almost giddy as they introduced caller after caller with stories of kindness in Edmonton.

I was finding this more and more irritating, for reasons I couldn't quite identify. One caller started in on a tale of the Kindness Elf, a twinkly being she had invented for her elementary school classroom, or maybe it was for her own kids—young children were involved in some way. "Fuck the Kindness Elf," I said aloud, fortunately alone in the car at the time, and snapped the radio off.

"Fuck the Kindness Elf"? What was that about, and why do I care if someone conjures up an admittedly treacly invisible elf who bustles around doing acts of kindness? I've been hearing a lot about kindness recently—injunctions to be kind, to practise kindness, in a world where you can be anything, be kind, and so on. I can't object to kindness as a practice in the time of Covid. What is my problem with the Elf?

My problem is that I am fed up to the point of anger with the relentless individualization of the Covid pandemic, as though it were fixable if we would all just do our individual part and be better people. Lack of kindness is not what got the world into this mess. Practising kindness is not going to get us out. Individual virtue and benevolence, as practised by the Kindness Elf, or the lack thereof, is not driving this catastrophe.

I'm reminded of something else I heard on the CBC, a day prior, which did not cause me to swear and turn the thing off. This was a talking-heads interview of the sort that I mentally classify as "peak public broadcasting," in which two professors were conversing about the problem of theodicy, and how eighteenth-century European philosophers worked and wrestled with it. The distinction between natural evil and moral evil emerged.

Natural evil, as I understood it, is that which causes suffering but has no human agent and results from no intentional action. Moral evil, by contrast, is suffering that arises from human agency, from the actions of those who could have done otherwise. Voltaire and (later) Rousseau argued over the 1755 Lisbon earthquake in this respect— was it a purely natural evil, in that the earth shook just because it shook, and not because anyone caused it to shake? Or were there elements of moral evil in the suffering caused by the earthquake, because the flimsily-built structures that collapsed on their inhabitants were the work of human hands?

I believe in the novel coronavirus as a natural evil. Nobody made it, and it doesn't have the capacity to act intentionally. It infects other organisms and destroys them as a means to reproducing itself, because that's what viruses do. We respond to natural evils through kindness and compassion, doing what we can to lessen the suffering of others. It isn't about justice or fairness or who did right or wrong. It's what we have to do.

Unlike a virus, however, a pandemic is not a natural evil. It's created and sustained by human action and human choices. Sometimes humans have no opportunity to refuse the actions that create pandemics: if you live in a shantytown with no clean water and cholera bacteria get loose, you're going to contribute to the cholera epidemic whether you intend to or not, just by living in your human body. The moral evil of your situation traces back to the people who eliminated everything except that shantytown as a place to live, and who made the decisions that meant that clean water was unavailable.

The moral evils of the Covid pandemic are many. I see Trump egging on his followers to ignore the danger of infection and gather in groups. I see Jair Bolsonaro denying that Covid exists. Closer to home, I see our premier denying, stalling and prevaricating about the virus because he wants to placate fringe elements who don't trust science. People have died because of these intentional actions. Maybe

Bolsonaro didn't wake up one morning and think, "I would like thousands of people to die. How can I accomplish this?" but he did wake up many mornings and refuse to do the things that would have kept those people from dying. The pandemic is all about justice and fairness and doing what is right versus what is wrong.

Returning to the Kindness Elf—when I hear or see or read about or am enjoined to respond to the pandemic in the register of individual kindness, with acts of person-to-person compassion, I feel the disquiet of misrecognition. It's not a lack of kindness that has brought about this disaster, but a lack of justice. When I see a moral evil misrecognized as a natural one, a bile of resentment starts to build up somewhere behind my consciousness, and some of it seeps out as "Fuck the Kindness Elf."

Practical kindness, kindness in action, has a different tone. Acts of kindness have been important to me. It's a cliché dating back to my days in church youth group that doing something good for other people really does help you to feel better about yourself, so for selfish and therapeutic reasons as well as altruistic ones, I consciously try to do nice things for people or to offer help when someone needs it. This is a tougher and I think more pragmatic approach to kindness than the damned Elf. Kindness is not enough. Kindness is not going to change what has gone very wrong. But kindness, at the moment, feels like the only thing I've got. I want to be an instrument of justice, but that is not available to me.

Like a Drug Deal

If you didn't know there was a pandemic on, you'd be forgiven for thinking that Edmonton is overrun with drug deals. With retail closed or severely limited, I find myself hanging around outside back doors or arranging quick handoffs of packages or waiting in my car for someone to drop the goods in the trunk and vanish back into their store. With the major vendors like grocery stores, click-and-collect is pretty routinized. With smaller ones, especially when I'm consciously trying to shop local, transactions have the feel of something that's happening outside normal commerce. Shops weren't set up for brief handoffs—smaller shops in particular were designed and furnished in order to persuade potential customers to linger, browse and admire. Covid has pared these transactions down to the minimum—I gave you money online, now you give me my groceries or houseplants or hardware as parsimoniously as possible and I'll leave quickly. These encounters feel vaguely illicit and improvised, even after eight months. This is how I often feel during the pandemic—I'm doing something that is somehow wrong but also somehow inevitable.

Hi Mom, It's Me

Yesterday I took part in a Zoom karaoke singalong at the seniors' residence near Toronto where my mother lives, with fifteen elders in little boxes on my screen. It was a cacophony of overlapping unmuted microphones, karaoke machine feedback, "Frosty the Snowman" and random jingles. I could tell from my screen that my mother saw me and sort-of recognized me, but was puzzled as to what I was doing there. I could see her gesturing, but couldn't direct her to use the chat box or to connect with me directly. In a moment of workaround inspiration, I clicked on my screen name and changed it from "MacBook Air" to "Amy Kaler Hi Mom It's Me." My mother's face lit up—she was sure who I was.

She made ear-cupping gestures and I realized she wanted me to call her. I picked up my phone and tapped in her number while watching her reach across her tray for her phone. I couldn't hear the buzz when my call came through on her, but I could see her phone vibrate. We chatted for about twenty minutes, our conversation mixing with the other strata of communication emanating from my laptop—karaoke, fragments of conversation, audio feedback, video bits of holiday decorations and tinsel.

These overlapping streams of input, at a great physical remove but enabled by screens, felt jarring and disorienting, a feeling that's become familiar over the past nine months of a pandemic that constrains social interaction. Talking to people, verbal communication, has gone from something linear and functionally pretty simple to something more intricate and punctuated. It's like going from mono to stereo sound, except that the experience isn't enhanced, it's degraded. It's also just plain weird to be watching my mother several thousand kilometres away going from on-screen bewilderment to semaphore to a voice emanating from my phone, all while "Frosty the Snowman" jolts out of my speakers.

Subtle Loss

It's almost the end of the first calendar year of the plague, so I'm seeing a lot of media stories about what we've lost. The losses that count in these stories are those that can be grieved, so this end-of-year stocktaking also invokes expressions of grief or sadness about all that was taken away. Some people lost a lot more than others—friends and family members, jobs, opportunities, finances, mental and physical health.

I'm thinking about two categories of subtle loss, which are so evanescent and insubstantial that they flicker around the edges of grief, producing a weird sort of not-mourning that manifests itself as disquiet and sadness. The first is the loss of the possibility that some of the bad things that happened this year could have happened in a better or more humane fashion. My father died in December. His death happened while he was alone, in an overcrowded hospital, with family members only able to say goodbye via FaceTime. He didn't die of Covid, at least not directly, and he might have died anyway in some alternate universe in which there was no pandemic. But in that alternate universe his death would have been different. It would not have been hemmed around by infection control protocols and isolation, it might not have happened in an underfunded and overcrowded urban hospital.

I grieve his death, and I also grieve the way it could have been, how his death might have been more humane in a universe without a pandemic. Both the fact of his death and the manner of his death are weighing on me.

I'm also mourning the loss, or perhaps just the absence, of my better self. As the pandemic has worn on, I have not become a nicer, warmer, more patient and more fun-to-be-around person. I may have become a wiser and more mindful one, but the jury is still out on the possibility of positive change. I'm watching, in real-time, the slow degradation of my important relationships because I am not the person I used to be (and neither is the friend, partner, family member or colleague in these relationships, because nobody's living their best life during a pandemic).

I'm grieving the slow going-away of that better and brighter version of myself. This is a weird thing to do, because the "I" who is observing this degradation is the same person who is no longer who she used to be. If that makes any sense. It's a subtle and confusing form of grief, this slow erosion of who I was and who I want to be, under the persistent quiet grinding of Covid.

Ice Is Solid and Liquid

The river changes constantly. It's winter and it's frozen, but "frozen" is many things. Near Dawson Bridge, the ice is chopped-up and partible, jagged slabs pushed on top of each other by the current, before the surface of the water slowly closed over and stilled, in the course of a few sub-zero days. It looks like a giant whipped pavlova or a trail of piercingly white construction rubble. It also looks stopped, but it's only stopped in the moment. Temperature and gravity and viscosity are still at work, and some day in the spring it will flow again.

I'm reminded of something I read about glass, that it is both solid and liquid at once. Glass is "kinetically settled" enough that its flow is infinitesimally slow, beyond the power of the human eye to perceive, but it is never entirely stable. It exists in a permanent state of slow motion. The river ice is like that.

I'm reminded also of the term "freeze-frame," referring to a photographic image that is motionless in the instant, but that exists only in relation to the frames that came before and after the freeze. It looks motionless, but it's part of an endless flow of becoming.

When I was walking southeast past the Highlands golf course on the riverbank, I heard a low soft boom, undercutting the hum of traffic. Something was happening on the river, under the ice surface. A big piece of ice, the size of a van, had shifted and was bouncing slowly off the chunks in front of it. I could just about see the outline of the dislodged piece. I knew it was going to move along down the river, but I didn't know where it would come to rest again, or how the river would be changed by its passing.

Rules and Vacations

I usually follow rules. I'm not sheep-like, but my working assumption is that if someone who knows more than I do made a rule about something, they probably had a good reason for doing so, so I default to the rule until I can figure out on my own whether the rule makes sense.

I also have a naïve belief in rationality and objective knowledge, which marks me as an Enlightenment subject, even though as a sociologist I should know better. I assume—again, not at the level of conscious thought—that when people do bad or stupid things, and they could have chosen not to do those things, they do so because they don't have enough information, or they don't know better. When you know better, you do better.

This pandemic has been hard on the rule-following, knowledge-trusting part of my psyche. Anger and frustration are part of my daily diet, exacerbated by accounts of people in positions of leadership who know better but don't do better, who break the rules because they don't want to follow them.

However, this is not my first rodeo, rage-and-frustration-wise. I've been here before, and I expect that you have too, reader, if you've had to deal with an addict or substance abuser in your inner circle. My civic emotions today, the dispositions I have towards my fellow citizens who are not following the rules, and my provincial government, which is enabling and abetting, map onto the craziness and toxicity of dealing with an active addict.

Addiction is characterized by deceit and self-centredness. Addicts say one thing and do another, and their behaviour is organized around protecting their ability to use their substance of choice at will. I'm not sure what the "substance of choice" is during a global health emergency, unless it is exactly that, individual choice, an addiction to being able to do whatever one wants.

I see the deceit and self-centredness playing out around following public health rules. These are effectively injunctions to abstinence, to asceticism: no parties, no social gatherings, no nonessential travel, no indoor recreation. No fun. No freedom. No wonder many people don't want to follow them.

When the public health injunctions started coming down from the provincial government, so did the exceptions to the rules. No indoor gathering—but if you're a church, it's okay, sort of, as long as you keep the numbers small. No house visitors—but over Christmas it's okay, sort of, as long as you don't have more than two visitors. In Twelve-Step lingo, the province had a case of the yeah-buts. Yeah, I'm going to stop drinking, but maybe just a beer every now and then. Yeah, I'm quitting, but after the holidays. Yeah, I'm putting sobriety first, but you can't really expect me to not have a glass of wine when people come over, right?

When the premier stressed how tough these restrictions would be, how much Albertans were going to suffer from not visiting their relatives or going on vacation, from one angle he sounded empathetic and humane, but from another angle, he sounded like he was, in recovery-speak, planning to fail. When the alcoholic focuses on how painful abstinence is and how horrible it will be to not have their substance in their metaphorical back pocket, it paves the way for the completely understandable relapses, the falling-off-the-wagon that is half-intentional. When an addict commits to quitting, and then veers off in search of allowable exceptions to abstinence and pre-emptive forgiveness for using, their primary commitment is not to a life without the substance.

For the people around addicts, this not-really-quitting is enraging. The addict looks sincere. They know that the substance is hurting them and everyone in their orbit. They sound plausible. They say the right words, over and over. They sound like reasonable people who understand rules and reasons. But they do not mean to stop using, not really. And they get found out, after they've done more harm.

Ice, Again

Again with the ice. The last two days I've been exercising a fascination with Mill Creek in its frozen state. The air temperature has been hovering just below freezing but many stretches of the creek are solid enough to bear my weight. In two locations just north and south of the Whyte Avenue bridge, I've clambered down through the deadfall to the creek's edge and stepped out gingerly onto the ice. Unlike river ice, the creek ice is frozen smooth and solid. It looks skateable, although I don't see signs that anyone has come down here for wild skating, away from the rinks and concourses cleared by the city for skating.

Standing on the ice and looking straight up the creek is something I could never do in summer. Walking on water, transformed by cold weather, I feel almost as though I were no longer terrestrial. I'm out of trees and brush and rocks, and onto a smoother, cleaner, simpler surface beneath my feet.

The creek marks a path through the brush, and I feel like I could move faster up that icy path than I could by meandering along the trails that wind beside it. I'm reminded of Joni Mitchell's song about a river you can skate away on. Leaving it all behind—skating away, skating out of here—is a very appealing fantasy in the ninth month of the pandemic, especially when I'm constantly reminded that I'm fixed in place for the duration.

And under the ice, the water. There is movement and fluidity under there—I'm not standing on a solid block. Something is happening under my feet as my gaze is drawn up the dull gleaming surface, dreaming of metaphors for escape.

Who Are You Going to Believe?

Covid is messing up epistemology for me. I am fortunate that I have not experienced it directly, and although I know people who know people who've been diagnosed with it, and even people who've died from it, Covid has not been in my home, here with me, manifested in heft and presence and undeniable embodiment. All I've got, when it comes to tangible proof of Covid, is the evidence of things unseen, and while that may work in matters of religious faith, it's unsatisfying as a basis of knowledge about a virus.

The pandemic appears in my life (or rather, doesn't appear) as an occluded threat. Nothing is on fire, no buildings are falling down, but at the same time everything has changed. The evidence of my senses—what I see, hear, smell—tells me nothing about Covid (and I hope Covid continues to evade my senses because I really, profoundly, don't want to have direct sick-person knowledge of this virus). I pay attention to communications and admonitions from authoritative sources and govern myself accordingly, in the absence of direct knowledge.

(I have an utterly absurd image in my mind of the Chief Medical Officer of Health for the province, who has been tasked with reminding, urging and imploring Albertans to take social distancing seriously, as Groucho Marx in *Duck Soup*, grinning roguishly at Margaret Dumont and asking, "Who are you going to believe? Me or your own lying eyes?" I'm going to believe you, thanks. I don't trust my own lying eyes in this matter).

I don't even have a direct image of Covid. For previous pandemics, visual representations have been present, for good or bad. HIV/AIDS, the only other pandemic I have experience of: skeletal young men in Manhattan hospitals, Freddie Mercury's final days, emaciated women and children in African villages. Sarcomas, wasting, gauntness. Covid—what does someone with Covid look like? How do they appear? The visual vocabulary of this disease has been so thoroughly mediated by medical technology that I can't see the face of the disease itself. If I run an image search for "Covid + person," most of the pictures that return are of medical personnel in head-to-toe PPE and Tyvek jumpsuits, or human figures almost hidden in a tangle of tubing and connections, faces covered by devices to help them breathe. The face of Covid is the face of technology, the evidence of human intervention already deployed to try to stop death.

I'm starting to feel nervous in public spaces when I see someone who has not been at least slightly modified by technology, in the form of a mask or face shield. But what does Covid itself—naked, unmasked—look like?

The combined invisibility/extreme visibility of Covid and its artifacts twists the boundary between what is known and what is unknown. I believe the experts when they tell me we're in the midst of a global health crisis, and not my own lying eyes when they tell me nothing has changed. For the past nine months I've been in this unsettling epistemological borderland, which is weirdly and not entirely comfortably reminiscent of my Christianity, to hold onto and abide by the evidence of things unseen.

No Time at the North Pole

My twin fascinations with extreme geographies and the warping of time have come together in a *Scientific American* article about time zones at the north pole, written by a researcher doing a stint on an American research vessel. As the lines of longitude, which make up the boundaries of the time zones, converge towards the pole, the barriers between the time zones collapse so that at the pole itself, in theory at least, it's every time at once. For people up there on ships, deciding whether it's eight o'clock or twelve o'clock is essentially arbitrary, with nothing to anchor their chronometry. And at the height of polar winters and summers, even the day-and-night rhythms of time passing are absorbed into a formless expanse of darkness or of light.

The author points out that this is different from the south pole, which at least has a continent, something firm underfoot, and a permanent population from different countries in different settlements, who usually adopt their national time zone as a matter of convenience. At the arctic end, by contrast, there's no "underfoot" because it's all ocean, and vessels can't anchor themselves as much as lock themselves into the slow flow of ice, drifting with that ice a few centimetres a day or a month.

That image of geographic and temporal formlessness fits the state of my pandemic mind. The spatial world has shrunk down to a few square kilometres (on some days, just the few square metres of my apartment), and the distinctions between places have evaporated. Home is work and work is home, the friends and colleagues on the other side of the planet are also in my bedroom one-tenth life sized, in little boxes on a screen, and I'm in their bedrooms too, or their basements or home office, all the while not actually going anywhere. The day-by-day serve-and-return of time passing has slowed to a halt as all days start to resemble the same day (facilitated in part by the absence of anywhere to go), yet there are still all the things I have to do, bobbing around in the hours and minutes. I haven't stepped out of time, because I still have tasks with which I mark that time is passing, but I've become distinctly unmoored.

Personal time, or little time, has become amorphous, and big time, public time, the time that gets measured in history, follows suit. I can't see what's ahead. I can't picture six months from now, or a year, or ten years. Will life go back to normal, with people reassuming their correct size and places, and the lights coming on and activity return- ing to the places that are now shuttered and silent? Or will the silence deepen, and will my future self be looking back at the self who is typing these words as one who is living at the beginning of the end?

When I try to imagine the future, I visualize a formless white field, like the frozen surface of the polar sea. On the white polar field, so I've read, our ability to gauge distance collapses. If you spot something moving, you can't tell whether it's just a few metres away or several kilometres distant. Is that black dot the size of a person, or the size of an enormous icebreaking ship? The horizon is at once impossibly close and impossibly far. And underneath everything, the ice keeps moving.

Getting Better or Not?

Things might be getting better. Alberta's Covid numbers have been stable for a few days; Trump is gone, and Biden is president. That's on one hand. On the other hand, the plateau that our Covid numbers appear to have reached is still sky-high, considered from the perspec- tive of just a few months ago; and while the occupant of the White House has changed, the threat of domestic terrorism and violence has been dialled down only a couple of notches, and the country is coming up on the half-million mark for deaths. I don't know what's going to happen. I don't know if it's going to be good or bad.

For a long time, not-knowing meant not knowing how bad things were going to get. I felt like a laboratory rat in some insane experiment, dumped in a maze in which every surface was electrified. Is the virus in the water? Will I run out of food? Are people going to die right in front of me, right on the street? Okay, maybe not that bad, but still really bad. Everything has stopped. There's no school. There's no travel. I have been within two metres of exactly two unmasked human beings in the last eight months. Is it going to get worse? How bad is this?

Now for the first time, not-knowing means not knowing how much better things might get. If the all-important numbers keep going in the right direction, maybe we'll have a real summer. Maybe businesses will open up. Maybe my daughter can get a summer job. Maybe I'll socialize with humans in person. Maybe I'll get off this damned screen. Maybe Biden can turn the country of my birth around. Maybe half a million deaths will be the last awful milestone.

And maybe not. A third wave could still happen, if not enough people get vaccinated in time (in time for what?). There are these new mutant strains. The rot in the United States may be too deep to be cauterized. This moment of slight optimism might only be a pause, not an inflection point.

I may have become habituated to crisis, so that the possible absence of crisis is faintly alarming, because it would mean not living the way I've been living for months. What I'm feeling, however, is not the trepidation or timidity of the lab rat whose cage door is starting to swing open, nervous about what lies on the other side. What I'm feeling is exhaustion, again, this time in the form of a half-deliberate blanking-out of the prospect of thinking about the future. I'm a lab rat who just wants to go to sleep in my pile of wood shavings and ignore the open door.

Thinking about a future that might be a good future, not a terrible one, turns out to be surprisingly hard work. I've learned to live with constant pessimism; adding optimism to the mix, without subtracting the pessimism, is an overload. I'm once again back to not being able to remember where I'm going or what I'm doing, why I'm standing in front of the open dryer or whether I've fed the cat today. In the last twenty-four hours, I've used the Find My Phone app on my iPad four times because I can't remember where I put the frigging phone.

I've had a sentence running through my mind, offering a bit of respite. It's "You do not require either belief or disbelief." I don't know where it comes from—it sounds a bit like it could be a life lesson from Harry Potter, also sounds a bit like some kind of pop Buddhist aphorism about nonattachment. Whatever the origin, it helps me to remember that no future, good or bad, needs me to believe in it. Optimism, pessimism, how bad it might get or how good it might get—these are epiphenomena of a particular set of cognitive skills that allow me to imagine futures that are not (yet or already or ever) real. They are not the guarantee of these futures, and so I'd better be sure I get them right.

I do not have to believe that things will get better in order for them to get better, and my disbelief is similarly unnecessary. I do not need to figure this out. If I'm tired, I can ignore the cage door, which may or may not be open, and instead burrow down and go to sleep.

Hard Freeze

Hard freeze last night, and today I went walking along the river west of Government House—not so much along the river as literally on the river, traversing a solid rubble-scape of ice. The question in my head: what time is it? Or more specifically, what kind of time is this? That question reverberated into two shapes, two amorphous cognitive spaces I'm trying to fill.

The first is the shape of historic time. How will this moment, in this pandemic, be remembered? We may be at a turning point. What significance is this moment going to bear when I look back, or someone not yet born, even, looks back? Am I living in an inflection point? A nadir, or the moment after a nadir, when things started to get better even though nobody knew it yet? Or is this the frontispiece to a story of even greater disruption, which I don't know about yet because as I'm having these thoughts it's only the middle of the winter?

The second is the shape I'm in, as in the title of Robbie Robertson's 1970 ode to despair, about looking at the water and thinking about jumping in. What are the qualities of this time? What am I experiencing, at the moment I'm experiencing it? What is it like to be almost a year into a global pandemic, maybe seeing light at the end of the tunnel but also maybe not? The future feels foreshortened because I don't know what's going to happen next month or next week. The present feels cyclic, as I find myself returning to dispositions, affects and disturbances that belong to previous episodes of calamity or stress. And the past feels very, very long. Ten weeks ago it was the beginning of November, Trump was president, and we were heading into a second wave that felt like a catastrophe, yet ten weeks is not that long in calendar time.

I'm thinking about time while tripping over frozen water down in the river valley, seeing the jammed-up angles of ice as arrested flow. The scientifically literate part of me knows that ice is a stage in the dynamic hydrological cycle—everything that is frozen now was liquid once, and will be again. It's just that I perceive this as stasis, with no movement forwards or back.

Falls the Shadow

Covid and time—it messes me up in the tiny micro-experiences of time, as well as on the grander scale of weeks, months, years, and what happened when. I've noticed in myself and others a new quickness, a rapid reactivity to perceived affronts, as though the time between the offense given and offense taken has been telescoped down to near-instantaneous. In other words, I am definitely more irritable, more on-edge, and more trigger-happy.

I've seen patience described as the opposite of anger, in both Christian and Buddhist religious writing, and what is patience if not the passage of time? If I'm more impatient now (and not coincidentally, more angry), that points to a disorder of time.

I used to be good at putting a buffer of time between the thing that happened and the way I responded to it, at least outwardly. Somebody says something or does something (or doesn't say or do something) that strikes sparks of anger—wait, count to ten, think about what I'm going to say before I say it. Allow time to slip in, separating the incident that happened and the way that I react. If emotional turmoil has been set off within me, put it to the side and give it time to subside. This is what people describe as being calm or thoughtful (or less flatteringly, as reserved and unemotional).

That buffer of time seems to have evaporated. I've come closer to snapping at people who may or may not deserve it in the past six months than I did in the preceding decade. It's not just me. I've seen explosive or semi-explosive interpersonal situations brew up suddenly, online or in person, with me in the role of onlooker. Most recently, a Zoom meeting of my university's governing body turned into a two and a half hour tempest of name-calling, interrupting and agitation.

There's something going on here with disinhibition, but there's also something going on with time. The weeks and months of Covid have slowed down, but the moments have sped up. Reactions are quick (and as I write this, I'm reminded that "quick," as in "cut to the quick," also refers to a site of painful, exposed vulnerability).

When I was a pretentious high school student, my friend-group got a bit obsessed with TS Eliot's *The Waste Land*. It portrays a state of lethargic, confused apathy, which is probably why it appealed to precocious Gen X teens. A snippet comes back to me, evoking paralysis and stasis:

> Between the conception
> And the creation
> Between the emotion
> And the response
> Falls the Shadow
> Life is very long

Life does indeed feel very long, and often very static. Time stretches out. But the Shadow—that period of time that inhibits the creation or the response—has disappeared. We're jolted immediately from trigger to explosion, from the spark to the blow-up, without the mediation or modulation of enough time.

Jellyfish Time

This pandemic is stealing time. I'm in my mid-fifties, so by any reasonable estimate there are more years behind me than ahead. I have plans for the years ahead—not so much concrete details but things I want to do, ways I want to live. And as this thing drags on towards its second year, I'm starting to feel my own years slipping away.

In some ways (many ways), I'm lucky. I consider people who are very young right now, for whom the year of the plague represents a much greater portion of their time on earth. For a ten-year-old, ten per cent of their life (and much more of their conscious life) has been lived under lockdowns and quarantines and the suspension of normal life. And these are formative years, crucial times of growth and learning, not just numbers on a calendar. The equivalent for me would be more than five years of pandemic time, which is beyond anything I want to think about. I've also had a lot of good years. If my life came to an end tomorrow, which is unlikely, it would not have been a boring life. But still, I want more.

The constant deferral of the pandemic—waiting until this passes over, waiting for the vaccine, waiting waiting waiting. "Constant deferral" ought to be an oxymoron, yet it feels real. As pandemic time grows ever longer, I can see the aspirations that I saved up for my middle age, and even my old age, receding until it looks like they're in danger of slipping past the vanishing point and disappearing altogether. Travel, learning new skills, volunteer work, some professional projects—am I going to get that time? I can occupy myself with long walks and making kombucha and sewing and plenty of other pastimes, when not in a state of acute stress or disorientation. But I don't just want time to pass, I want to possess it. I want to *have time* for the things I want to do, but that time is receding from me. I don't have it. I might not get it.

The image that comes to mind, completely bizarre as many of these pandemic metaphors are, is of trying to scoop up a jellyfish or an anemone or some amorphous but living creature that keeps slipping through my fingers and slithering back into the water. I want to hold onto time, make it solid and vibrant in my hands, but my hands are still only empty.

Walking into the Hill

A few days ago I walked through the person-sized culvert running under 76 Avenue where it dips down into the ravine. I had walked up the creek from Whyte Avenue, enjoying the slightly surreal feeling—look, I'm literally walking on water! The culvert appeared as a black hole in the hillside. I considered climbing up and around but decided to go through.

It was a bit of a reckless decision. The tunnel of the culvert is slightly curved, and is long enough that I couldn't see the light at the far end. It was also pitch dark inside. The ice had been frozen for a long time, but I had no guarantee that I wasn't going to drop through a softened spot in the dark and end up waist-deep in icy water.

Despite my better judgment, I really wanted to find out if I could go through that culvert. Perhaps I was thinking that if I could walk on water, surely I could disappear into a hill and emerge on the other side. It would be a bit of minor magic, like something that a secondary character from CS Lewis or Tolkien might do. So I went in.

It was not the first time I'd done something dumb or dangerous in the ravine. In the midst of the constraints and privations of the pandemic, the river valley activated a bit of anarchism that was dormant in me the rest of the time, a desire to push limits, to go where I wasn't supposed to go and do what I wasn't supposed to do. This was not an anti-social urge—I had no desire to shoplift or spray graffiti—it was an urge to step off the path and explore, to expand my sense of self from a timid and high-anxiety being into someone adventurous, who pushed through bushes just to see what was on the other side, or who scrambled close enough to the edge of the drop-off to see what was directly below.

So—into the hillside. There was enough space to walk upright, but not much more. I couldn't see what was in front of my feet, so I inched forward keeping one hand on the wall of the culvert. The ice was smooth as glass, protected from snow. My feet met no resistance at all. From many years of urban life, I had an association between holes in infrastructure and odours I didn't want to smell, so I had a small reflexive aversion to breathing too deeply—but it's winter, it's far too cold for anything unpleasant to thrive on the walls, keep moving forward.

The walls themselves were the surprise. As I got closer to the other end the light started opening up and I saw that the walls were luridly, ebulliently graffitied. They effloresced with a motley of shapes, images and words, so vibrant that I half-expected them to glow. This was graffiti to a much higher standard than I had encountered above ground, including both official murals and the walls the city had designated for that purpose.

I saw a few instances of the huge genitalia and wannabe gang signs that I might have expected, but more than that, I saw abstractions in purple and orange, swirls of green and red and rust, ghosts and pirate ships, mathematical equations, and aphorisms. I saw "EVERYTHING AT YOUR OWN RISK" and "BE GAY DO CRIME." Someone, or a collection of someones, had come in at their own risk and done some small crimes with spray paint and stencils. The vibrancy contrasted with the solid white of new snow outside, stippled by black and brown leafless trees.

Shuffling forward and snapping a few clumsy cellphone pictures, I made my way to the other end of the tunnel. From the outside, I could see a date over the lintel—the tunnel had been there since 1932. The graffiti I saw in 2020 might have been layered over other painting and doodling from the last eighty years. In many parts of the world that wouldn't constitute a broad sweep of time, but in settler Edmonton, eighty years is an epoch.

I would never have seen this cavern if I hadn't been emboldened by the experience of walking on water, imbued with the desire to see what was out there, to see whether I could walk into a hill. I was primed for the little risks of travelling into the culvert by the experience of subjugation to the much bigger risk of the pandemic, a risk that I couldn't control or mitigate. For a few minutes, in the culvert, I felt like an explorer, a person who went out and found something new in the world, a respite from being a person whose life was circumscribed by avoiding a virus.

Moon Illusion

Linear or progressive time has been missing in action for quite a few months now. I don't know what's coming next, so I pay attention to what's coming round again, and again, and again. I'm experiencing a lot of recursions, returns and cycles. The repetitions of the natural world are oddly soothing, and I find myself seeking them out.

Changes in seasons move slowly enough that day-to-day shifts are rarely noticeable, but the phases of the moon provide a nightly encounter with cyclical time. Pre-pandemic, I rarely knew what phase the moon was in; now it's part of my consciousness. I'm starting to understand in a visceral way why ancient cultures marked the year by lunar cycles. I want to understand how this works, how the moon swells and shrinks and swells again.

Last week I watched the moon ascend over downtown Edmonton, across the North Saskatchewan River and the Mill Creek ravine. Moonrise was fast and lovely, the moon getting smaller and smaller as it cleared the horizon and swung up into the night sky.

Everything in that last sentence is untrue except for the loveliness. The moon does not rise—the earth turns beneath it. This memory comes to me from an elementary-school science project, a Styrofoam earth with a pencil for an axis, a lightbulb sun, and a compact mirror moon, the earth swivelling on the pencil as the whole contraption swings around the bulb, the Sharpie mark on the globe signifying "you are here," turning away from the light moving into the dark. In grade four, I understood why the moon appeared to climb up over the horizon.

What fourth-grade science could not explain is the matter of the diminishing moon. I know the moon could not actually get smaller as it rose, but my eyes persist in seeing a big silver disk metamorphosing into a tiny disk as it ascends. Because I have a dilettante's interest in astronomy and a more existential interest in why we think things are true when they are not, I typed "why does moon appear big" into Google.

The most important thing I learned: no one knows why the moon looks smaller as it rises. This phenomenon is called the "moon illusion," and it has preoccupied scientists and philosophers for thousands of years. Twenty-three hundred years ago, Aristotle ventured that the earth's atmosphere possessed some quality that magnified objects at the horizon, just as it filtered colours, making the moon appear orange or red. A thousand years ago the Iraqi physicist Ibn al-Haytham theorized that the moon illusion was actually a psychological phenomenon, with the moon's diminution residing in the minds of the observer rather than the properties of the moon itself.

Variants of this psychological explanation took hold, and in the past two centuries physicists have speculated that the moon looks big near the horizon because it's in the same visual plane as things that we know to be big, like tall buildings or mountains. When it rises, or appears to rise, out of the horizon and into the depthless and disorienting sky, we no longer see it as large-by-association.

Another explanation: our minds register the moon as a large object because experience has taught us that objects on the horizon that appear small may actually be very big. A moving van ten miles down a prairie road occupies a smaller slice of our visual field than a moving van twenty feet away, but we know that both vans are the same size. We unconsciously apply this correction to the image of the moon. In this account, the moon illusion is a learned response—babies or the newly sighted, perhaps, would see the moon as its true size, not diminishing as it rises.

The moon illusion is remarkable because it is one of very few optical illusions that arise spontaneously from the workings of natural forces, requiring no human interventions to set the stage or arrange objects in a particular configuration. Other well-known illusions such as the converging train tracks or MC Escher's staircases folding in on themselves, are the obvious products of human artifice, organized so as to suggest that one element was larger or smaller or equivalent in size to another, even though measurements of inches or centimetres or handspans showed that what appears to be so was not so.

The moon illusion, by contrast, is not human-made. It was not created as a question for the eyes, with rulers or calipers or yardsticks providing the answer. The moon illusion is the natural world offer-ing a mystery with no answer. The moon says: your eyes are faithless witnesses—they report what is not there, so that you see but you do not truly know. It says: your acts of observation—watching the moon get smaller as night wears on, or remarking to a companion that the moon is especially large and round tonight—are in fact acts of creation, as you invent the thing that you believe you see. You can't trust the evidence of your eyes.

Time Dividend

Time, again. Too much and not enough and not the right kind. I'm accustomed to time as a scarce commodity. I'm used to having more to do than I have time to do it in, first as an anxious overachiever in childhood and undergraduate days, then as a teacher, then as a profes-sor, and concurrently as a single parent. These are all occupations in which nothing is ever perfect, in the archaic sense of the word signifying completion. If I just had a few more hours or days or weeks or years, whatever I'm doing now could be so much better!

In the days before the pandemic, when I had so much work to do and not enough time or space to do it in, I used to dream about controlling time. I had a recurring fantasy about being able to pause time for the world around me, allowing me to step out of the flow for long enough to finish writing everything I needed to write, getting things ready that needed to be gotten ready, get emails lined up and ready to send, take care of domestic tasks, maybe get a little time for leisure—and then press "play" and restart the flow of time.

Before Covid, one of my keenest mundane pleasures was the discovery that I had more time than I thought—I've already prepped that lecture, that deadline isn't for another month, this thing that I thought would take an hour only took fifteen minutes. There was pure happiness in *saving time*, which I suspect was not so much about me saving time as about the feeling that time had saved me. Those extra moments, along with all the things I could do in them, were going to save me from mediocrity or from some obscure form of failure. Saving time felt like wealth and virtue. (I am very aware of how deeply this orientation to time is embedded in a specific cultural formation I have inherited, a particularly Protestant anxiety many generations deep).

During the pandemic, many of the things that demanded my time were subtracted from my life, first suddenly, and then bit by bit, draining away. After the first frenetic few weeks in March and April executing an improvised pivot to doing all my work online, pulling together a framework for my daughter's online schooling, and rushing around stocking up on isopropyl alcohol and gloves, eventually there seemed to be less and less to do. My workplace was closed, so no commuting. Meetings with students and colleagues—after the first few months, no one really had the energy for more than the bare essentials. My volunteer and community work was on indefinite hold. Switching over to remote teaching, recording lectures and class materials, was excruciatingly painful at first, but the pain came mainly from having to figure out how to do a lot of new things with inadequate resources, not from having to put in two or three times as many hours.

Approaching the first anniversary of the shutdown, I find that I have time. There are entire days on the weekend when I don't have any fixed engagements. I have things that must be accomplished, but I don't have the same cage of schedules, appointments, what must happen at this specific moment on the clock. When I read what other people are writing about this moment, "time soup" seems to be the term of art.

So now I have time. But I don't feel like I used to imagine I would feel, if I had been gifted with additional hours and days. If you'd asked me how I would feel about getting a lot more time, I'd have imagined it as a fertile field, ready for me to scatter the seeds of those ideas and aspirations and projects that had been indefinitely deferred by more pressing events, and fertilizing them with care and attention and watching them grow.

But in reality, now that I have time, that's not happening. This extra time is barren. I can't grow into it, turn it into hours and days that will flower forth with achievements. It does not have the feel of abundant potential. I've been starting projects but not finishing them, I've been thinking about the things I could do—acquire advanced cooking skills, start training for a half-marathon, clean the whole apartment from top to bottom, but can't find whatever divine spark I need to move ahead with them.

I'm not getting much done. I'm aware that I'm wasting time. I'm letting it pour through my hands and down the drain of Covid. But I'm too anxious to stop wasting it. I can't pay attention, pay heed, well enough to invest this time into something productive.

Because I can't spend this time well, my dividend of extra hours and days doesn't present itself as abundance but as inadequacy. If time is money, as all the foregoing metaphors suggest, the time that I've gained in the past ten months is foreign currency that I can't spend and can't convert into something more valuable. It's the handful of creased and faintly greasy euros and Ethiopian birr and Sudanese pounds and Chinese renminbi that have been mouldering away at the back of a desk drawer, worth something in theory, but in practice not really. I can't exchange it for something better, swap worthless time for good time.

I have too much time, but it's not enough, and it's not the right currency. I can't use it and I can't save it either. If I can't make this Covid-time useful, I can't ever be at rest in it.

Adolescent Bardo

Thinking about pandemic irritability—the flareups of indignation because someone is where they shouldn't be, doing what I don't want them to do, making my life difficult, getting in my way. Why isn't my grocery order ready? I called it in three hours ago! This student who wants to know what's on the midterm should just read the damn syllabus and stop wasting my time. Oh hell, that slow-moving neighbour with the yappy dog is at the communal mailboxes. Is she planning to take all day to look at her supermarket flyers? I don't want to talk to her, and I definitely don't want to hear that dog. Why can't she keep it quiet? These little eruptions punctuate a vast swath of ennui, waiting for...something. It's like apathy and impatience at the same time, two states of mind that shouldn't coexist, but they do.

In these erratic swings between fatigue and irritation, I see again that pandemic affects are returns to previous states of mind, recursions of sentiments that were laid down in earlier life, like water flowing back into old channels. I'm thinking that the way I'm feeling now recapitulates adolescence.

I know I've been here before. Surges of annoyance coupled with recognizing the annoyance is far out of proportion to the trigger, intense ambivalence about being around other people, awkwardness when I do encounter other people in real time and live-and-in-person—when did I first encounter this state of being in the world? All the years between twelve and eighteen, that's when. I had some good times as a teenager, but most of it was spent wanting to be somewhere that is not here, waiting for I didn't know what, wanting something to happen to make everything better, but unable to zero in on the things that could effect this transformation.

Adolescence was a kind of bardo, an uncomfortable and sometimes excruciating wait for deliverance. When I feel this anger that goes from zero-to-sixty in a flash, or moods that swing wildly and independently of what's happening in the here and now, I can almost feel the ratcheting up and down of emotion, with a keenness that I haven't experienced in decades. The exact hormones and brain chemicals involved in producing adolescent snappishness and boredom have long since run their course with me, but there's got to be something neurochemically weird happening now as well, in this prolonged absence of social contacts, the arrival and withdrawal of the hope that this isolation will end soon. Once again, I find myself waiting for real life—adult life—to begin, and not being entirely confident that it's going to go well.

This return to adolescence makes a certain weird sense—the habits and dispositions of a successful achievement of adult life have been vacuumed away by isolation, so where is my consciousness, and my unconsciousness going to go? Back to the time before I acquired all those dispositions and habits, back to the days when life was like an eternal waiting room, with the fluorescent light buzzing and the uncomfortable chairs, and everybody getting in my way just a little too much.

Proprioception

Today the Facebook Memories feature let me know that I've circled around the sun once since the most severe physical injury of my adult life. This injury happened in early 2020, just as news of this strange virus in China was starting to permeate my consciousness, and in retrospect perhaps I should have taken it as an omen.

Last winter I had an unfortunate incident involving a toboggan on steep slope in the vertiginous western edge of the river valley. I was out with my daughter and her friend and her friend's mother, and at the urging of the teenagers, I took a fast ride down a slick and icy stretch of hill. It ended abruptly when I ran into a tree and did some significant damage to the lower part of my right leg.

Fortunately, the friend's mother is a physician. She told me that nothing looked obviously broken and that I should probably not bother with the emergency room, because showing up on a weekend evening with an injury that was neither life-threatening nor easy to treat would mean a very long and uncomfortable wait. She and the teenagers helped me to hobble to their place nearby, where I managed to get my boot off before the rapid swelling locked the boot into place on my leg, and we made our way home later, me thoroughly dosed with painkillers and in possession of compression stockings and a tensor bandage.

My leg got a little better over the next few days but not much, and the swelling didn't go down, so I finally gave in and went to my doctor, who referred me for imaging scans. There I learned that the technical term for what I did is a complete severing of the posterior cruciate ligament, and what that means in practical terms is that the lower part of my right leg had, and still has, a much more tenuous relationship to the rest of my body than is ideally the case.

For several weeks after I managed to do this to myself, I had trouble getting around. I was hyper-conscious of my halting ability to walk, and of my slowness and of the pain that could flare up if I stepped the wrong way. So I went to see a physiotherapist, who tapped and prodded me and asked if I could put weight on my right leg. By that time, it had been long enough since the accident that I was able to say, "Yes, I can bear weight," and to hop gingerly on my right foot a few times to demonstrate my point. He asked again, "Do you feel like you can bear weight?" Yes, I said, you just asked me, and I just showed you. No, said the physiotherapist, "I'm asking how it feels. Do you know what's going on? Can you sense what's going on with your leg before you actually step downwards on it, do you understand what's happening?"

I realized then that he was talking not about function but about sensation and about awareness. Did I know where my leg was in space?

The answer, unfortunately, was no, not without looking at it carefully. The physiological term for this is proprioception, and my proprioception with respect to that part of myself that had been injured was thoroughly screwed up. My grounding was tenuous. I was uncertain about where I was stepping because I didn't have a sense of where my leg was without looking right at it. Evidently the nerves that transmit information from my brain to my extremities and back again had been so disrupted that the messages weren't getting through. Over time, they might rewire themselves, but in the meantime I had a proprioception problem.

Translating this proprioception problem from the realm of the spatial to the temporal realm brings to me to pandemic time. Over the first few months of Covid, I lost the ability to determine where or when I was—not in the sense of being able to name the month or year, because that could be fixed just by looking at a calendar, but in the sense of being able to determine how near or how far I am relative to other events in the flow of time. I couldn't feel the distances of time. How long ago did something happen? Was it recent, or buried far off in the past? Is an upcoming event imminent, and therefore very close, or way off, barely discernible from my position in the centre of now?

My experience with disruptions in physical proprioception, brought about by falling down a hill, gave me a way to name my experiences with time, and how I could no longer feel myself in relationship to past and future. In a very strange way, my awareness of myself in the flow of time was like my right leg, extending carefully and uncertainly towards what has already happened and what is yet to come.

Lost Places and the Annual Lockdown

Two days ago I was interviewed for a three-minute TV spot about the possibility (more than just possibility, a strong likelihood) that Alberta will go into our second consecutive spring lockdown because cases of the new Covid variants are doubling, quadrupling, and threatening to explode. I know intellectually how exponential growth works and what it means when case counts are doubling every seven days, but the sheer numbers involved always blindside me. The possibility (probability?) that in a month's time we could be right back to November, to the terrifying and vertiginous surges and the white-hot intensity of the emergency rooms and field hospitals causes something deep inside me to drop heavy and fast.

The TV journalist's pitch was "can we make lockdowns great again?", summoning, with a sardonic gesture to American politics, the enthusiasm and novelty of the first spring lockdown, with backdoor concerts, nightly pot-banging to encourage healthcare workers, and the proliferation of new home-based hobbies among the comfortably housed. Invited to look back on those days, part of me wants to sneer. Look at those fools (including me). They really thought this was going to be over soon. It might never be over. We might be reliving these ups and downs, the rise of cases, the fall of cases, the optimism, the defeat, over and over again.

Under the sneer, the sadness. When the reporter asked me how we could get through the next round of lockdowns, I had to pause. I literally did not have words. The pause seemed to go on for much longer than a simple gathering of thoughts should have required. Eventually I came up with something about gratitude lists and that was that. I am really not sure I know how to talk about the possibility that this is not anywhere near over.

Later that day I had to go out to do errands of the sort that have become mundane—call ahead to the grocery store to arrange to pick up an order, gauge how crowded the parking lot is before going into Canadian Tire for more masks, stand outside the front door of the library and call the librarians so that my books on hold can be brought out and dropped on the holds table in front of what used to be the main entrance, find the coffee shop with the drive-through as a reward on the way home. None of these are particularly onerous.

Getting them all done meant circumnavigating this small city, however, which meant I was constantly reminded of places where, pre-pandemic, I might have lingered a bit. I passed the university, where my office has been unoccupied for a year, and the coffee shop where I used to be able to sit with my laptop for hours, as a sort of second office, now with tables and chairs stacked against the walls so that only swift pickups and takeouts could happen. I used to browse the stacks in the library, now I don't.

My interactions with places, the webs of connections and the registers of engagement with my surroundings, are being stripped down to the simplest and more functional activities—get it done, get out. I was never much of a flaneuse, but I do embody memories of a less linear and more digressive way of moving through the city. I remember the smell of my office after the cleaners had been through, the light reflecting off the spines of plastic-jacketed library books, the automatic mist spraying over the panoply of fresh vegetables at the grocery store.

The pandemic city, the probably-just-pre-third-lockdown city, feels like a geography of loss. It's a geography of straight lines, flat planes, and the shortest distance between two points. Moving through the world used to be more diffuse and digressive. I used to inhabit these places with more presence and more intuition than is available to me now. All the possibilities of work, leisure, provisioning, have shrunk down to what can be done at home. The geography of loss has become a geography of less, of living with restrictions and smaller spaces, of living without the richness of places out there in my city.

My geography of less is not a geography of deprivation. I am nothing if not adaptable, and I'm lucky, compared to many others, because I've still got a job and work that I can bring home, and because my home-place can expand, albeit awkwardly, to accommodate the diminished forms that leisure and provisioning now take. Nonetheless, travelling around the city I feel as though I've lost places, just as I seemed for a very long moment to lose words in the interview.

Spring 2021

Two Futures

Once more I'm seeing the pandemic future forking in front of me. One fork leads to a pleasant country on the far shore of this turbulence, where the vaccines have worked their magic, everyone's had their shots, and I'm a person of alternating busyness and leisure again, riding elevators with other people from meeting to meeting, deciding which of the many possible coffee shops I will attend to do a bit of reading before my graduate class consisting of live human bodies in real time.

The other fork leads to another turn of this wheel we've been strapped to, another shutdown or confinement or whatever it will be called, because the virus variants have gotten out of control, we didn't act quickly or decisively enough to prevent them from multiplying, and it's the second pandemic spring and summer and no coffee shops, no classes with live people, and no elevator small talk is on the horizon.

My imagination can race down either fork in this trail—the fork it chooses is determined by the news sources I've most recently paid attention to. If I tune into to the optimism station, everything's going to be okay. We have remarkable vaccines. They are being deployed. All the elderly people in Alberta's long-term care residences are going to be vaccinated very soon, and the queues of ambulances with sirens silenced outside the doors of seniors' residences, the doors themselves stippled with caution tape, those will soon be things of the past. At the top of the news: we are going to be okay. We've come through. It's almost over. The future is so close, we can almost touch it.

But if I turn the dial on my thought processes, literally or figuratively—everything will not be okay. On the pessimism station, the epidemiological projections show the variants swelling inexorably, taking on the visual appearance of a tidal wave on the graphs, because they multiply so fast and are so much more contagious. The vaccine is too little, too late. We are going to be back to stacked-up gurneys and bodies wrapped in plastic before the geese return in the spring. It will be like the fall, except even more demoralizing and grim. Everybody I know will get sick. I can't do this again, but I will have to do this again.

I can't hold these two futures in my mind at the same time. I can't look at them both and think, "well, it might go this way, or it might go this other way." This inability is frustrating. By now, sure, after how many months, I should be used to indeterminacy and to not knowing what's going to happen, I should have cultivated the ability to coexist with uncertainty, yet I have not. I am certain about one future in one moment, and then I'm just as certain about the other in the next moment. If I think too much about this overly-flexible quality of my certainties, I feel that old epistemological vertigo coming on, that sense of groundlessness. Yet the vertigo doesn't stop me from trying to parse it out, trying to figure out, with the limited tools available to me, *what is going to happen.*

I don't want to believe that the future really is unwritten, that it is unknowable and inaccessible except by living through it. If I read enough, if I listen enough, if I pay enough attention, I will be able to crack the code. The idea that "it could go either way" is even more destabilizing than the broadcasts on the pessimism station.

Brain Studies

It's been long enough since the riots on Capitol Hill in the US at the beginning of January that psychological profiles of the rioters are beginning to emerge, drawing on the copious social media postings and contributions of the rioters. Once again, anger and Covid are twined together. I was struck by a *Washington Post* article about one man named Michael Sparks, who generated a stream of explosive Facebook and Twitter accounts of his radicalization before he took to Washington.

Sparks isn't particularly significant as an individual for what went down on Capitol Hill, he's just well-documented. What drew my attention was the way he describes his rage and anger towards what he perceived as threats to the white Christian way of life. He uses the language of conviction, obsession and addiction, fed by social media consumption. He was self-aware enough to know that spending all his time on extremist Facebook pages was not healthy, and was in contradiction to his Christian beliefs in peace, even as he justified his anger as religiously sanctioned because his freedom of worship was allegedly under attack. But he couldn't stop scrolling and he couldn't stop clicking and he couldn't stop raging.

I followed up citations in the article, which drew me into academic papers on the neurobiology of anger, an obscure field that has become almost shockingly relevant in the past year. The researchers confirmed the impression from the *Post* article of a person in the grip of a wired-in compulsion. In the words of researcher James Kimmel Jr., "Your brain on grievance looks a lot like your brain on drugs...harboring a grievance (a perceived wrong or injustice, real or imagined) activates the same neural reward circuitry as narcotics."

The opportunity to behave ragefully—to burn a building, to send a nasty tweet, to get into a street altercation with someone—offers the same kind of release that using narcotics does for the person addicted to drugs. And after the building is burnt, if the grievances continue to be stoked, the craving for release builds up again, and the anticipation of the pleasure to be found in burning another building, sending another nasty tweet or getting your aggression out with another person on the street send the rage-addled person out to find that release.

Kimmel and colleagues describe this as revenge addiction rather than anger addiction because it's the acting-out part rather than the emotion of anger that fuels the cycle of compulsion (and also, I suspect, because revenge is easier to cloak in moral or ethical respectability than aimless Incredible-Hulk outbursts). Surges of dopamine are released in the parts of the brain that respond to external rewards and pleasures, which means that people who are particularly strongly motivated by reward are also particularly vulnerable to this grievance-rage-attack-relief cycle. Constant exposure to things that make you angry can literally change your brain (and unfortunately constant exposure to things that make you angry also generates lots of click-throughs and revenue for social media giants, so Facebook and Twitter have no interest in dialling down the extremism and fury that populates the nether reaches of their platforms).

The pandemic was implicated in Sparks's descent into revenge-addiction. He believed that Covid restrictions were interfering with his family's freedom of worship, and that the pandemic was being used as a Trojan horse to import alien values from antifa and the Black Lives Matter movement into towns and cities across the country. He saw Covid as part of "spiritual warfare" being waged against people like him.

None of this was news to me—the idea of "spiritual warfare" against the corruption of liberalism has been floating around for years, and as a sociologist I know all about strain theories of violence, which hold that when people experience frustration because the resources and opportunities they have access to are incommensurate with their expectations, the strain of holding experience and expectation gets resolved in violent acting-out, often described as venting frustration. And the pandemic has been one long exercise in having experiences wildly out of synch with what most people want from life.

But the idea that this has a physiological component—that you can look at the brain of someone who got angrier and angrier over the course of the pandemic, and goaded by the extreme right, developed a compulsive drive for revenge that can actually be visualized on a brain scanner—that idea stopped me in my tracks.

How many other people out there have been neurologically changed by the pandemic, and by the perverse pressures it exerts on vulnerable reward circuitry in the brain? Are the street-level interpersonal displays of aggression and short temper that I've been observing for the past eight months driven by a sort of hydraulics of compulsion, similar to the compulsion to use narcotics? I knew that in these outbursts there had to be something going on beyond just lowered thresholds of impulse control; could this rage-compulsion be it? Have neural pathways been permanently deformed by the pandemic, so that we're looking at years of people chasing the retaliation-and-revenge high, driven onwards by anger wired into their brains?

And then the question I really don't want to think about—if the pandemic is changing Michael Sparks's brain, is it also changing mine? I'm not prone to rage, but what other forms is this rewiring taking? Am I changing in ways that will prove durable, and I don't even know it?

Skiing

I bought cross-country skis a few years ago as part of an effort to make some sort of peace with the winter. I'd heard many people say that if you can walk, you can ski Nordic-fashion, and after a few outings managed to get myself moving in the right direction. I never got the trick of the swift glide, but did achieve a sort of continuous lunge, which smoothed itself out enough that I could enjoy the trails, the wind in my ears, the dazzling white. Until Covid, this was the main way that I used the river valley trails, for ski outings a few times each winter.

I didn't know it, but I was pandemic-ready. This year, I've read, cross-country skis have become almost impossible to buy as people in Edmonton make a massive pivot to outdoor recreation, so I'm fortunate that I already had some.

Today I took them to the Highland Golf Club for the first time. The tracks had been groomed on the weekend, but it was just above freezing, so the curving runnels in the snow were interspersed with patches of grey slush and the yellowed tips of last summer's grass. This is probably one of the last good skiing weekends of the season.

It was almost silent. I passed a few other skiers, with what I think of as a Scandinavian mien—grey-haired, thin and wiry, Fair Isle sweaters with high socks and wooden poles. They're out on the golf course to cover ground, not to see and be seen. When I heard the shushing of skis coming up behind me, I hop-stepped out of the tracks to watch them go by. I saw a few arctic hares too, white on white, distinguished from snow only by the slight blurs of grey around the muzzle. It was a peaceful scene.

Yesterday I was in a skiing scene that was not so peaceful. I had decided to take some adult fundamentals-of-Nordic ski lessons, hoping to correct my self-taught awkwardness. The group met at Gold Bar Park, in the area known as "the grid"—a series of practice tracks laid out in parallel near the parking lot, where aspiring skiers could practise strides and glides, sliding back and forth like beads on an abacus.

It was a warm day after two weeks of bone-chilling cold. Everyone was out. I don't think I've seen that many people in one place, outdoors, with intermittent mask use, since last winter. Maybe if I had a dog and had been going back and forth to the dog park for the past year, I'd have gotten more used to crowded outdoor spaces. Little kids were bobbling along in snowsuits, some of them towed on toboggans by older siblings or parents, weekend warriors were getting in everyone's way with their shiny new gear and officiousness, and the ultra-proficient speed-skiers were zooming in and out of the trees, in reflective goggles and shiny tight Lycra bodysuits.

The ten of us in the adult fundamentals class were trying to listen to our coach, who told us to drop our poles and "listen to your feet," to let the skis become part of our embodiment. We kicked, glided, fell down every few minutes, got up and out of the way, got back in the tracks of the grid and went back and forth. Occasionally a stray dog or child wandered across the grid.

The scene was festive. It was like one of Edmonton's winter festivals from the time before Covid, with people out on a sunny wintry day for no reason other than a good time. What came to mind, however, was not the memory of good times past but the notion of Mardi Gras (helped perhaps because we're into the second week of Lent). Mardi Gras is associated with debauched revelry, and while nothing could have been more wholesome than the people milling about with their kids and dogs and skis and poles and tiny backpacks, the scene to me still held a tinge of licence, a faint aspect of rule-breaking. I was reminded, bizarrely, of carnival, the site where inversions of the normal orders of life are sanctioned and deviance, whether mild or extreme, is celebrated and encouraged.

There was nothing remotely licentious about Gold Bar Park on Sunday morning, but it felt faintly off. The past year has tinged the idea of gathering in groups with the faint sense of danger. Something risky is happening here—the virus could be out there, what looks like fun on the surface could be the means of delivering sickness.

This is what public health messaging has told us, and what I have taken on board. I know that the configurations of people on a weekend morning at Gold Bar are okay. I know that the virus isn't supersonic, that it's not going to leap from a toddler in a crash helmet and mini-skis to a once-and-future Olympian swooping around the curves of the track. But something inside me has been conditioned by the pandemic. My perceptions have been changed such that when I see groups of people mingling, even in a setting as benign as an outdoor park, my first, unthinking, response is to kick up the vigilance by a notch or two. They're too close to each other, or they might get too close to each other, and some of them aren't wearing masks. This can't be right.

I have to take a mental step back and look at the situation again, consciously engaging my knowledge about viruses and transmission. It's outdoors, the wind is blowing gently, people are in motion, no one is hanging off anyone else in an alarming fashion. Everything is okay. With a conscious effort to ground myself in the reality of the situation rather than in the muddy vagueness of fear, I'm able to appreciate what I see, and to appreciate the fact that I'm out here too, on this sunny Sunday.

The vigilance doesn't completely drain away, however, and that is why I prefer the silence of the golf course on a weekday afternoon, mushy tracks and all. When the pandemic ends, how long will it take until I'm not slightly tense around even minor crowds?

This Is Your Brain on Covid

If I were running a year-long experiment on the effects of immersion in prolonged risk and ambiguity, I'd be writing up results around now. By this point in the pandemic, I've learned to recognize the cognitive tax of Covid in a thousand daily ways—forgetting where I put my keys, prolonged moments with fingers poised over keyboard as I try to recall what I was planning to say—but I'm also noticing subtle effects when I contemplate the not-quite-unthinkable future—that the pandemic will be over someday, and life will change. Specifically, I can't think myself into that future, as a better, happier post-pandemic version of myself. I fear that I'm stuck with the Covid-warped version of me.

I'm worried that the pandemic will change but I won't. When I imagine the future, I see myself still harnessed to the habits of being that sprang from the pandemic—hesitant, risk-averse, peripheral to social life, a bit of a grey wraith. This doesn't make sense. There is no reason to assume that I won't adapt to post-pandemic life just as I adapted to the pandemic, but I can't shake the image of myself as insubstantial as smoke, never again fully present even when Covid restrictions are eased.

I think I have an instrumentation problem here. I don't have the right tools for the task at hand. I'm trying to think about the long-term effects of a pandemic-addled mind, using that same pandemic-addled mind to think with. (I realize I'm tracking into Cartesian dualism by distinguishing between my self and my mind, but for the sake of argument, I'm going to leave it as is). I have the capacity to picture a post-pandemic world, but I don't have the capacity to see myself in it. I can't execute the subjective pivot from observer to observed in my fantasy of what will happen once the vaccines take hold.

I try to imagine myself going to church, meeting students, teaching in person, doing things with friends, working for hours in a coffee shop, and all I see is the grey wraith backing away from human contact, clinging to the peripheries. I can't imagine myself as fully competent, plugged in, filled with *élan vital*. I see myself instead as someone who isn't up to it, whatever "it" may be: teaching, grant-writing, volunteering, the give and take of good conversation.

This bothers me, because I used to be up to it, in fact used to be able to cut a pretty good swath through the world. The possibility that I might be permanently diminished by the pandemic is frightening. My inability to place myself into the future as a fully competent person is both alarming and depressing. Am I going to be like this, neurasthenic and reclusive, forever? Permanently distracted, avoidant, easily confused?

I remind myself that this inability is a barometer of my present condition, not a reliable predictor of my future. Right now, I may not be capable of imagining the good version of my future self, while I'm still subject to the strains of the pandemic present. My mind is not as deft as it was a year ago. Immersion in uncertainty, risk and threat has damped down my imaginative capacity, as all my energy or electricity or glucose or animal spirits or whatever you want to call it has been diverted into managing a state of constant vigilance.

I'm fortunate that I don't suffer from anxiety in its really bad manifestations, such as sleep disorders or the inability to eat, but the forces of chronic stress and anxiety are working on me nonetheless. Mental depletion assumes the form of the impossibility of imagining myself as anything but depleted. I can picture the future, I just can't muster the energy to imagine a subjectivity other than the one I inhabit right now, one that is much closer to the grey wraith than I would like.

I've read a lot of commentary on the pandemic by theologians and historians who keep circling back to the moral and spiritual disturbances named by eremitic wise men and women who lived, by choice, lives of isolation and renunciation. Acedia, a toxic concoction of lethargy, apathy and cynicism, seems to be having a moment. Presbyterian writer Kathleen Norris wrote an eerily prescient book a few years ago, *Acedia and Me,* which is now being cited by psychologists. An article naming acedia as "the emotion we're all feeling right now," by a Catholic historian specializing in early monastic practices of asceticism, has been circulating around my friend network for months.

In addition to acedia, I'd also like to revive the concept of akrasia, which predates Christianity, but which slipped into early theology around the same time as acedia, through the influence of Aristotle on Augustine. Akrasia is the feeling of being unable to do what one should do, of knowing that actions need to be taken but being unable to call up the self-mastery or self-control needed to actually make a move and take those actions.

I learned about it through a book of conversations amongst a psychiatrist, a philosopher and a Buddhist monk called *Freedom for All of Us*. Despite the somewhat saccharine title, as I read it I could feel the gears clicking into place in my mind, as I received the words naming my inchoate distresses. Practices of freedom, say the monk and the philosopher and the psychiatrist, are what bring healing from akrasia. These practices need not be outward assertions of autonomy or choice, but can be enacted completely within one's mind. I admire this in theory, but in reality, in the grinding boredom and uncertainty and strangeness of the pandemic, I am far from freedom.

Covid has brought akrasia on me. Moving forward, whether in physical action or in the workings of the imagination, does not feel accessible right now. I know what I need to do, yet I don't do it.

Ravine and Downtown

I went down to Mill Creek ravine to walk today, but encountered setbacks and switchbacks. It was a warm Saturday afternoon. I was heading north on the trails, but many people walking many dogs were heading south, requiring me to thread my way through retrievers and labradoodles.

At one point I was stalled behind a group of four teens who were ambling ahead of me, laughing and poking at each other with sticks. I wanted to pass them but wasn't sure how—do I yell "on your left!" as I would if I were biking? Or just scramble past them through the snowy spruce to either side of the path? The etiquette of pandemic proximity in the outdoors still isn't entirely fixed in my mind, and I'm never sure how much space I'm supposed to give people, how close is too close, how not to inadvertently provoke alarm by crossing an invisible barrier of air.

I moved off the main trail to a smaller and more tortuous one a bit higher on the bank of the ravine, but there I encountered the mountain bikers weaving their way up and down the very narrow path at high speed. A mountain bike headed at me or coming up from behind doesn't give me time for pondering the etiquette of physical distancing; I just had to leap out of the way. This began to irritate me intensely. These are *my* trails. Shouldn't a pedestrian hiker have precedence over an expensive fat-tired machine? Why do I have to give way? I want the right of way!

I realized that my preoccupation with manoeuvring around other people and my fussy inner monologue about their rudeness were working against the tonic of my ravine walks. I still felt like I'd been deprived, however, and wanted a treat. I remembered that a book I had ordered had come in a bookstore downtown.

Downtown is a ten-minute drive. It was also nearly devoid of people, except for a few individuals with the motley look of people experiencing homelessness, hefting overstuffed backpacks or pushing shopping carts. Broad avenues were pocked with empty and boarded-up storefronts, and drifts of snow blew past a few overflowing garbage bins. Stores were open but silent—no one going in or coming out, no gusts of cinnamon-scented air from the bakery as the door swung open. The bookstore was all but closed—the front door was locked, and I had to call from my side of the window to the employee sorting through bins of books on the other side. I thought this was odd, then realized that bookstore owners probably don't want anyone to browse, especially as the only people out on the downtown streets were people who had nowhere else to go.

I collected my book, reaching through the cracked-open door, and drove home, contemplating the contrast between the peopled wildness of the ravine and the barren commercial streets of the city. The places where people are and the places where people are not— these are no longer what they used to be.

The Place Becomes Strange

This afternoon I was on the north side of town, driving through the Oliver neighbourhood to pick up work supplies at Staples. I stopped at a crosswalk to let two elderly masked women cross. My attention was caught by a notice taped to a tree next to the car. I'm always drawn to messages for the general public, searching for a lost pet or a roommate for a two-bedroom apartment, quick glimpses of private lives dropped into the public view. Years ago, cities like Edmonton seemed to be festooned with notices on every available surface in densely populated neighbourhoods, but the internet has swallowed up most of the seeking-and-offering, closing down these little vistas of the lives of strangers.

This notice was hand-printed in block capitals, giving it a look of improvisation or of urgency. I couldn't read everything in the few seconds before I had to move the car forwards, but I could tell it was about a car crash that had occurred at this intersection, and a plea to anyone who had might have been present and seen the crash to call the number on the poster. Whoever put up the poster was in need of a witness.

Somebody had gotten hurt there. I didn't know who that person was (and never would, unless I called the phone number and outed myself as someone who knew what happened). For someone, that intersection, where 116 Street crosses 102 Avenue, is now marked as the place where harm happened. For somebody, or possibly several somebodies somewhere in Edmonton, this has become the site of the bad thing.

I was conscious, as I have been so many times during this pandemic, of my proximity to the danger that befell strangers. I've made my way through the year relatively unimpeded, trudging along like the old women for whom I stopped at the intersection, knowing that I needed to be careful but determined to get to the other side. But not everyone crosses safely at the same place. This place, like so many places in Edmonton, holds histories that would have remained unknown to me were it not for a notice on a tree. This route, which I've travelled probably hundreds of times since moving to Edmonton, became a little bit strange, a little bit unrecognizable, made so by my new knowledge of the crash. The pandemic has heightened my consciousness of the moments of transformation, when the familiar becomes uncanny or even dangerous.

The previous day, I'd had another experience of my familiar places transformed, in a more benign fashion. Every year in Mill Creek ravine, the local francophone association holds a three- or four-day festival called the Flying Canoë Volant. This is best appreciated at night, when the valley and the surrounding residential streets light up with lanterns in the trees, tents and tipis glowing from within. The ravine is taken over by a sort of domesticated Mardi Gras spirit. Neighbours emerge and wander in packs past the outdoor stage, the ice slide, the hot cider stands and fire barrels and maple sugar snow moulds, while interpreters costumed as *coureurs de bois*, in black and red checked shirts and long red stocking caps, wearing half-scale canoes suspended from shoulder harnesses, weave through the crowds declaiming folk tales about flying canoes, in both official languages. It's civic-minded, wholesome, and often very cold.

This year was unseasonably warm. On the last night of the festival, I went out with two friends to check out what the Flying Canoe would look like in the time of Covid. Almost all of Edmonton's abundant festivals have been cancelled, and this was my first visit to a public happening in a year.

It wasn't the same as other years. It wasn't worse—just different. I had to book in advance to register the three of us, so that the festival organizers could avoid crowds. Because it was dark with only a new moon, I brought a flashlight so we wouldn't skid or trip in the wooded slopes where the tree lanterns marked the path. I couldn't see more than a few metres in front of me, but I did not see many people in those few metres of light that moved as I moved. I spotted the outlines of small clumps of people here and there, further up the trail, in twos and threes rather than the jovial bands of friends or family that crowded the festival in previous years. The experience was a bit more mysterious, a bit less boisterous. At the risk of sounding sentimental, I would say, however, that it was a bit magical after all, the first public magic I had experienced in a long time.

At one point as we headed downhill towards the frozen creek, I realized that we were on one of "my" paths, and had been for about half an hour. In the daylight, this was a hiking trail that took me in and out of the spruce groves on the east side of the old rail bed, but at night, in the dark, with luminescent trees, it had become subtly strange. "My" paths, and my ravine, were not really mine. This place, which I had invested with my own energy and meaning on many afternoons of walking, walking and walking, was a different place, drawn into the circle of the festival by night. The stories that I had conjured out of it were mine, but the place itself belonged to everyone, to me and my friends and the other scattered strangers on the trails. After a year of semi-obligatory isolation, shading into solipsism, I've started to forget that the small world I've drawn around myself has other citizens besides me, even if we don't acknowledge one another.

The next morning, I walked out on the ravine path in daylight. The festival was over and the site crew were taking down the decorations and installations, with elaborately choreographed and physically distanced reaching, unfastening, dismantling, carrying and loading of objects into golf carts. They looked tired. They probably were tired. The remnants of the festival looked odd and a bit surreal. Many things were where they should not be in harsh daylight—canoes wedged in trees, giant opalescent mushrooms looming over benches, electric wires trailing from branches. On my way back home I retraced my steps and was mildly relieved to see that that the canoes were out of the trees and the visual incongruities had been resolved. Things were back in place.

Life on Mars

I've been listening over and over to the first audio recordings sent back by Perseverance, the rover that landed on Mars last week. For the first time in history, the sounds of another world. The sound itself isn't that extraordinary, just some creaking and faint whistling of the Martian wind blowing past some metal bit of the rover. But the pure alienness of it keeps me coming back to these few seconds of audio file, clicking the replay button on my screen.

No one has ever been farther from what they hear than I am from the Martian trills. No sound has ever been farther from a hearer. That enormous distance between the cold Martian wind somewhere on the red planet and me listening to it in a sunny spot by a window in Edmonton is an experience of the sublime. I remember flying over the continental divide and looking down at the mountains from the aircraft. I was always amazed by how much land there is and how few signs of people, once you get north of the populated belt near the American border. The mountains and lakes and land going on and on forever, unwitnessed, unobserved and untouchable.

The fragments of song from the rover on Mars partake of the same vastness. Yet somehow, it doesn't evoke loneliness for me. The sounds speak to me of the beauty of distance and isolation, not of my own smallness or insignificance. I've become attuned to that kind of beauty in a way that I was not before the pandemic. My interest in extremity, rigor, and the absence of people that I've honed through reading and in an earthbound way through walking and exploring has brought forth a capacity for amazement that was never there before. I could listen to the sounds of Mars all day.

Leonard Cohen at the Whistle Stop Café

I took a course in developmental psych as an undergrad. I was captured by the idea of children's moral development, that there are many ways to respond to a situation in which harm may happen to someone and we learn new ways and let go of older ones as we grow. Because we're a social species, both children and adults also judge other people's actions in the presence of harm as right or wrong, but those judgments are contingent and local to a place, a time, a set of influences, rather than absolute.

This resonates with life-as-it-is: I experience personal morality not as something that I have already achieved and perfected, but as a constant shuffling amongst positions and values, some of which, in hindsight, I am more proud of than others. Self-righteousness is a particular tripwire, as is a tendency towards rigid judgments. I strive for a supple but strong foundation on which to build an understanding of what is right and wrong, but so far "strong" seems to prevail over "supple." All of which is to say: I am judgy as heck and I don't know whether that's a good thing.

The pandemic is, amongst many other things, a cornucopia of opportunities to exercise moral decision-making, and to watch with admiration or horror the exercise of the same by other people. In the moment that is now, when we are not yet to the other shore of the virus, the moral decisions are about how to behave in a world that contains other people. Do I wear a mask if nobody's watching? Do I elevate my wish to see friends and family in the US to a must-have and fly south for the winter? Do I send my kid to school when she's coughing, and I have to show up at work or risk getting laid off? Do I implement hospital triage protocols and remove the breathing tube form the elderly man with COPD so the ventilator can be attached to the young woman with severe silent hypoxia?

This moral landscape of Covid is going to change soon, maybe as soon as this summer. Alberta is still knee-deep in the middle of the river of infection, but thanks to vaccines I can make out the far shoreline. I'm thinking about what I'm going to do when I get there, and especially, who's going to be there with me. And when I think about the people who are there with me, I'm going to be thinking about the choices they made. And this is where I get extra judgy.

To be specific: on the far shore there are going to be people (let's call them "us") who've done our best to not spread Covid and to look after the fraying fabric of individual and collective well-being, and there are also going to be people who went to anti-mask rallies and piled into vans to caravan to diners and churches that break the rules, like the Whistle Stop Café in central Alberta, which has been much in the news lately for its owner's defiance of public health restrictions. Contemplating people who claim that there's no virus and who dispar- age people like me who are in a state of high alarm over the virus, I feel like I'm trapped in one of Leonard Cohen's more dystopian moments, the song titled, bleakly, "There is a War," which describes a world of ambiguous and free-floating hostilities between the people who believe they're in a war and the people who believe there's no war.

The ones who say there isn't a war—no virus, nothing to fear, we're going to live our lives without the burdens of masks and two- metre distances and arrows on the floor—will be on the other side of the river, when I get there, and I doubt they will have been particularly chastened by the rough crossing, if indeed they noticed it. They've been buffered by their version of life-as-usual, by a year of eating out and socializing with friends and leisurely shopping, with a few anti- vaccine memes passed around for a bit of frisson.

What am I going to do about these people? Since I'm not in a position to actually do something to or about or with these people, the question is really: how am I going to live with my judgment of them? What am I going to do about my certainty that there is something very wrong here, that some of us paid and paid and paid (more than I had to pay), and some of us worked and worked and worked (more than I had to work) to hold the virus off, while others just had a reasonably good time and can now say to anyone who's listening, "We were right.

Lockdowns aren't necessary. Restrictions aren't necessary. 99% survival rate, no worse than the flu. Freedom wins!"

What is the most morally evolved response to this situation, for those of us who knew there was a war? Constant anger at the injustice of the pandemic is not going to make the peace. There are places and situations in which anger is the fuel we burn to get things done, but that's not true all the time, and like most combustible fuels, anger is toxic if you ingest too much of it. And the future, which will contain these people, is very long.

How do I reconcile with this future, knowing that there is no outcome that will suit my not-so-highly-evolved desire for a justice that provides rewards for the people who did the right things—and punishment or at least very awkward public shaming, for the ones who didn't? I know you can't always get what you want, and Cohen's oeuvre tells me that nobody gets what they deserve, but I also know that sometimes, whether by grace or by luck or by work, you do get what you need. In this moment, in the post-pandemic jumble of anger and patience and impatience and hope, I think what I need will be found in the work of rebuilding, once we get to the other shore.

So many things fell apart, or almost fell apart, and will need to be held together. So many things went dark, or not quite dark yet, and we will need to turn the lights back on. Friendships, workplaces, life's work, equanimity, communities, faith, politics. If you haven't experienced how broken something is, you can't grasp the importance of the work of repair. If you haven't seen our collective well-being, or science or rationality, as something worth preserving, you also haven't seen the lights that we're turning back on. It's not enough, but it is something.

Cohen's most overquoted line is from his song "Anthem," about the crack in everything, the one that lets the light get in. However, Anne Lamott points out that the better line in this song is one that comes before the famous one, about ringing the bells that still can ring. Coming through Covid, doing the best I can with the light available to me, is like being the bell or the ringer or both. For the past year, we gave much of our lives over to Covid, shutting down the socializing, pulling back into home spaces, withdrawing to wherever we could find. Some of this sacrifice was voluntary—we could have chosen to do otherwise—and some was not.

This is what I'm holding onto as the world lurches into whatever comes next. There will be anti-maskers and virus-deniers, who claim there was never a war. But our moral reasoning need not be the same as their moral reasoning, and there is no requirement that we reconcile the two. We may not get what we want, which would be some form of Olympian justice for those who behaved badly, and we may also not get the future we deserve, but we will get what we need. I don't need to spend the post-pandemic being self-righteous, and I also don't need to spend it being bitter (although I'm going to hang onto the option of anger, because anger gets things done).

We are the bells that still can ring, and all the little bits of light. It will always have been worthwhile.

Desolation

It's been very cold and now it's unseasonably warm, and snow is dissolving into muddy brown water. Two weeks ago the river valley was starkly beautiful, if a bit terrifying, but now my trails are just sloughs of grey slush. The trash of the fall and winter is slowly coming to light, with discarded masks prominent amongst the flotsam. I went down in the valley to walk because I wanted some inspiration, and I came back without any. It's an ugly time of year. In a few more weeks bits of green may start emerging from the tips of branches, but today the idea of spring and the return of life seem very far off.

There's news on the vaccine front—the province has a surplus of one particular type of vaccine and it's being distributed to people in my age group. The vaccines are better than anyone could have hoped for, and they appear (for now at least) to be effective against the mutant strains of Covid that are arising in the city, even as the case counts for the original coronavirus go down. So I might be able to get immunized sooner rather than later, and the immunity from Covid might be real and durable. I might be able to get the shot soon, or get an appointment for the shot, and thereby take one giant step out of this ugly and grimy pandemic time.

Or I might not. The appointments are being scheduled by year of birth, and by the time my year comes to the front of the line, the supply of vaccine might be used up. I want vaccine shots to go into as many bodies as possible, for the healing of the community, but I also want a vaccine shot to go into my very specific body, and that might happen or it might not. This might be something to look forward to, or it might pass me by. Also, the vaccines defeat the variants for now, but what about a month, six months, a year from now? What I feel in this moment isn't really optimism or anticipation. There's a flicker of hope, to be sure, but there's also a lot of dull greyness that is not hope.

A word rose up in my mind—desolation. When a word comes to me so strongly, I want to know why. I checked the Oxford English Dictionary to find its history.

"Desolation" originates from the Latin *de solare,* which can be rendered as "to make [something] completely alone." "Solare" means the condition of being alone and the prefix "de-," which in other words may mean the opposite or the negation, here means "totally and completely." It is related to, although opposite from, solace or consolation.

Desolation is a feeling and it's also a place, an actual literal place on the map of the world. The word and the place have been lingering in my mind because of my childhood fascination with Antarctica, which has become reactivated during the pandemic.

Antarctica is as close to another planet as it is possible to be—no cities, no farms, nothing green or warm, and almost no people, except for a handful of scientists. A line through the centre of Antarctica would strike the equator at an exact right angle. At the pole, east and west and south disappear and the only possible direction is north.

And just off the Antarctic coast are the Desolation Islands, also known as the Kerguelen Islands (I was about to say—off the northern coast, but every coast is northern). These are wind-battered bits of rock, officially part of the French Southern and Antarctic Lands, with an official population of zero. They are not entirely deserted—there are a few French scientists staffing a research station and, according to the internet, packs of feral cats descended from the mousers of nineteenth-century whaling ships. The indigenous fauna are limited to a few migrating whales and seals and a permanent presence of animals with names that are almost comically unappealing: the Patagonian toothfish, the spiny lobster.

The Desolation Islands are cold, dangerous and far away, but they are not entirely removed from humanity. In 2019 UNESCO declared the French Austral Lands and Seas, of which these islands are part, a World Heritage Site. UNESCO proclamations describe the islands as "one of the last wilderness areas on the planet" as a consequence of their "great distance from human activities." Nonetheless, says UNESCO, "Grandiose volcanic landscapes teeming with life reinforce the exceptional character of the site. These territories stimulate the imagination and are a source of inspiration to anyone."

So. Desolation, the place, is not simply emptiness or void. Even there, living beings are moving. I picture one of the French scientists slipping out of the temporary buildings that comprise the monitoring station to walk the beach, perhaps at the early sunset of the Antarctic winter, perhaps finding some sort of inspiration from the rocks and the sea and the absence of any conventional points of reference.

On the opposite end of the planet, desolation recurs. Cape Desolation is a point off the southwestern coast of Greenland. It may have served as an overwintering spot for Erik Ericsson in the tenth century, and nineteenth-century whalers navigated by it. No one lives there and no land animals are evident. But like the Desolation Islands thousands of kilometres to the south, Cape Desolation is not entirely devoid of life.

In 2014 Canadian scientists doing hydrological research encountered a coral reef off the cape. Equipment they dropped into the water to measure temperature and speed came back smashed, with bits of pink and white matter hanging off it. "At first, the researchers were swearing and cursing at the smashed equipment, and were just about to throw the pieces of coral back into the sea, when luckily, they realized what they were holding," said Helle Jørgensbye, a student on the research team. The coral making up the reef thrive in dark and deep water, and they may have been building their living walls, unseen and unknown, for eight thousand years. In Europe to the east and north America to the west, civilizations rose and fell while the coral, in the cold and silence, kept working.

Desolation, both the mental state and the places, seems like somewhere I've been during this pandemic. My mind on Covid has its Kerguelen Islands and Cape Desolations, remote from any system, any community, any network of thoughts and ideas that would enable me to believe that I had a place in an ordered world. My desolation came on even as human-to-human interaction shut down, despite my immersion in a world of internet technologies that promise connection, gratification and purpose.

Desolation is not the answer to the question "who am I?" It is the place where that question is asked. The only answer—the only consolation—is the one that I give myself. The only boat that could take me from the shores of desolation, and in which I might return, is the one that I built myself, out of twines and scrubby trees and roots that grew stubbornly on the salt-washed shores.

My scrubs and trees and roots were the conscious desires to assign value to my circumstances. They were small things, minor credos I invented (every day, walk a little, read a little, write a little). They were rituals I invented because I needed a ritual, not because of any transcendent purpose.

During the pandemic, when most of the external structure of work and school and church went away, these self-directed rituals grew in significance. These practices are not as superficial as fads or fashions, but neither are they as deep or coherent as a life goal or a transcendent purpose. They existed at a mid-level, between the semi-intentional small actions of trivial life, and the grander and more reflexive life projects. They were the homemade rafts that I strung together out of scraps of good intentions.

Sometimes these minor practices coalesced around an idea, a theme, something that was important because I decided to make it important. The Zoom meetings with people I knew from high school or from church exist because I decided to favour bridge-building as a mode of engagement with others, pushing beyond my innate insularity. The masks I made out of curtain scraps and the kombucha I brewed in a pickle jar exist because I decided to favour bricolage, making something out of the debris of other things. The walks and hikes I took in the river valley happened because I decided to favour being in a place, being in this place, rather than just passing through it, especially once I couldn't go anywhere anymore. This manuscript that you are now reading exists in part because I decided to favour creativity, which meant writing even when I didn't know if I had anything to say.

All these efforts, all these bits of moss or twigs build the coracle in which I may circle the Kerguelens, although I don't yet know when or if the virus will let me leave. When that day comes, I may bring all these bits and pieces with me, tie them all together with some living fibre, and tip them into the cold ocean to form a new reef. This is where I was, during the Covid-19 pandemic. I was out here in the cold water. But I did not drown.

Spring 2021   143

Coda

Vaccine Theology

One month after the first anniversary of Covid, on April 15, I got my first dose of the AstraZeneca Covid vaccine in a tiny storefront clinic just north of Edmonton's downtown, empty except for me and the pharmacist. The procedure took eleven minutes, from walking in with a requisition on my phone to walking out with a proof-of-vaccine card, including five minutes sitting on a plastic stacking chair, waiting to make sure I wasn't going to go into anaphylactic shock. In the intervening minutes, half a millilitre of AstraZeneca, consisting of genetic information for a coronavirus spike packed into a chimpanzee viral vector, went into my upper right arm. I walked into the clinic as a body at risk of sickness or death from the virus and I walked out a few minutes later as—well, not exactly not-at-risk, not until a few weeks after my second dose, and even then, no vaccine is one hundred per cent protective—but at least on the way towards immunity, inflecting the curve of my own vulnerability and bending it towards safety.

My unconscious mind has a flair for the dramatic, and programs the inside-my-head soundtrack accordingly. Leaving the clinic, lines from Handel's Messiah ran through my mind: "...the trumpet shall sound/and the dead shall be raised incorruptible/and we shall be changed." I was not being raised incorruptible, but something had happened. My body was being changed. I didn't look any different from the outside, but inside me, something was present that was not present before the shot.

This subtle yet consequential transformation was produced by a literal laying-on of hands, as the pharmacist steadied the hypodermic on my right shoulder before pushing in the plunger. I imagine that he repeated this ritual dozens of times that day, as strangers one after another entered his pharmacy seeking not just the vaccine but release from the anxiety that one might contract Covid oneself, or the guilt that one might infect someone else. We came into the pharmacy in one condition and left in another, with the assurance that we could begin to unburden ourselves of the weight of living as a potential Covid-carrier, the weight of wondering whether or when we might start coughing and not be able to stop.

That night, twelve hours almost to the minute that I received the vaccine, I woke up feverish, aching, and shaking, as though frozen to the bone. Waves of heat and cold swept over me, and I realized that I could control the shakes in one part of my body through concentration, only to lose control over what was going on elsewhere. I knew that I might have side effects with this vaccine, but had rather arrogantly assumed that I wouldn't because I had sailed through other vaccinations, for flu or shingles or hepatitis, never experiencing anything beyond mild soreness. This was extremely different. I got the complete shipwreck, crossed with malaria and a good helping of the Twilight Zone.

In the middle of the night, beset by tremors, I somehow formed the thought that I was in physical shock, that the shaking was caused by a sudden drop in blood sugar, and that therefore I needed to consume something sweet as quickly as possible. I wondered if I could get to the fridge, where there was a can of maple syrup. For a moment, this seemed like a good way to self-medicate, until I realized that it was not. There was no shock, no external crisis cutting into my ability to regulate my blood pressure or glucose levels. There was no problem. It was just the AstraZeneca, mimicking a coronavirus invasion, mobilizing killer T-lymphocytes inside me, generating inflammation as it did so. This wasn't something that was happening to me, it was happening in me.

In a slightly delirious way, I was glad of the sturm und drang manifestations of an immune response ramping up. It was evidence that something had happened, evidence that I was being changed. Probably because of the same fever reasoning that led me to believe I needed to eat a lot of maple syrup from the can, I started recalling episodes of *Doctor Who*, specifically the final show of each season, in which the Doctor, with maximum histrionics and drama, dies to his old self and is instantly remade as a new self, the Ninth or Tenth or

Eleventh Doctor, the same person and yet not at all the same. Because my life is not a BBC production, there were no spectacular visible transformations into David Tennant. But I was being altered by the vaccine nonetheless. The person who came out on the other side of vaccination was not entirely the same person as the one who went in.

I'd spent much of the past year in the uncomfortable spaces between solidarity and aversion when it came to interacting with others. I was profoundly connected to my communities in ways that I hadn't been conscious of pre-Covid, through shared air and breath, but my community was also entirely imaginary, as I hadn't gone anywhere near any living and breathing people if I could avoid it. This shot was the first sign that I might be able to get out of that space and re-enter real time and real life with other embodied people.

Eight weeks later, I got my second injection. The injection itself was unhurried and undramatic, anticlimactic really. Nonetheless, I had a brief attack of dizziness watching the pharmacy technician prep the needle. It felt like some sort of reversal, or a turnaround in a flow, dropping momentarily into an aporia before resurfacing.

I've gotten used to these momentary vertigos during Covid. They are always about something other than low blood sugar or not drinking enough water. What was this one about? The first-order answer to this question is always "Covid fatigue," yet each instance of fatigue is a bit different.

In this case, it's about the fourteen months of working on managing the boundaries of body and mind—what to let in, what to exclude, reject, repel? For more than a year, the watchwords for personal health have been isolate, separate, exclude. Keep the droplets out of your face, keep the contaminated air out of the indoors, keep the people out of the schools, churches, workplaces, and ultimately, as much as possible keep everything and everyone out of my space. I evaluated technologies and practices by how well they kept things out—double masks versus single ones, HEPA filters, capacity limits, filtering people into groups of close contacts (and not so close contacts, and people who were too far away to be contacts in any meaningful sense). When in doubt, no contact is the best contact.

I had to do similar work in the world between my ears as in the world outside my head. From the first days of the pandemic, information, mis- and dis- and otherwise, was flying around, fast and erratic, like a swarm of drunk hornets. The virus is in the water, you can get it from the slipstream, masks protect you, masks cause asthma, Bill Gates, biowar lab in Wuhan, vitamin D, kids don't get it, kids get it but don't get sick, kids get very sick, P-1, blood clots, natural immunity, hygiene theatre. Some of that information was true and useful, or a reasonable approximation thereof, and some of it was—not. Factually incorrect, mistaken, "motivated reasoning" or lies, can you tell the difference? I couldn't, not at first. And so, for months one of my major mental tasks was to determine what information to let in, what I would allow to shape my beliefs and actions, and what I would exclude, keep out, push away from my consciousness and back into the hive of bad faith or ignorance that it flew out of.

This sort of mental border maintenance carries costs. I'm reminded of adenosine triphosphate, the molecule in all living cells whose job is to carry energy from sugar and carbohydrate stores to the cellular operations where the energy is needed and ensure that nothing that isn't needed crosses the membranes around those operations. Transporting energy across membranes is work in itself, burning up energy in the making and breaking of molecular bonds, to ensure that sugars are allocated properly for the cell to function. Mobilizing energy within a cell is much more laborious, in a chemical sense, than just spreading through a medium, like dropping ink into water and watching the colours diffuse.

I'm conscious of the work that has gone into moving information around. It takes attention and deliberation to bring the good knowledge in—can I trust this source? Is it logical? Is it consistent with what I know to be true? Is it observable? Bringing the good information in would be meaningless if weren't twinned with the work of keeping the bad information out, a constant separation of sheep from goats.

Keeping out homeopathy, conspiracy theories, 5G and bleach and skewed statistics is work too, especially during the initial open and receptive, anxious, what-the-hell-is-going-on phase of the pandemic.

Here is where the borders of the pandemic mind map onto the boundaries of the pandemic body. Both boundaries are defended and patrolled during Covid. (It's not for nothing that the spread of conspiracy theories was called the second pandemic, or the infodemic). For mind and body, for the duration of the pandemic, the best self is the most strongly bounded self, not the diffuse and permeable self, through which viruses and bad information can drift in without resistance. When in doubt, keep it out—people in your living space (except for the designated close contacts), virus particles in the air, ideas from QAnon.

And then, vaccination. If science were capable of irony, this would be ironic. The logic of vaccinating, the best hope of getting out of this pandemic, runs counter to the logic of the physically and mentally protected self. Hypodermic injections are boundary-crossing, as the words "injection" and "hypodermic" themselves make plain—this stuff gets into you, under your skin. Vaccines are transparent liquids that literally go right out of little glass bottles into the muscle of your upper arm. They have an unsettling corporeality after so many months of keeping all things visible and invisible outside your body. If immunity could be conferred by bathing in an infrared glow, or passing through a fine mist that sheathes you with an extra layer of protection, such an intervention would be more consistent with the exigencies of the past year than a shot in the arm.

Because the vaccines are really effective, getting vaccinated means that the work of sorting out what is dangerous from what is safe, what will help and what will hurt, can be ramped down, although it's never going to go away completely. The energy that went into this work of sorting and selecting and maintaining boundaries will gradually start to dwindle, or to go back into storage for the next crisis. Getting vaccinated may not be the end of the pandemic, but it is the end of something. Covid fatigue is losing its potency, and that instant of vertigo in the strip-mall was the mark of its passing.

At the beginning of the pandemic more than a year ago, I knew I didn't have Covid because nobody I knew had Covid and there was no way I could have contracted it. I was definitely Covid-negative, uninfected. Then, as the weeks and months went by, came the possibility that I might not stay that way.

Being uninfected is different from being not-infected-yet, and it was the not-yet-ness that I came to occupy during the first year of Covid. For twelve months, I was living in the in-between of sickness and health, walking around in a body with the potential to become infected. And so was everyone around me.

And also: asymptomatic infection. Would I know if I were infected? And—at the point where health becomes ethics—if I were infected, did I pass that infection on to someone else, and never know it? The morning after the night of the side effects from my first shot, I did some internet reading about vaccine reactions, and learned that there may be a loose association between strong reactions to the shot and having had a mild or asymptomatic case of Covid. Had I been infected months ago, unaware?

I'll never know if I got Covid without realizing it. I might have been infected and been entirely unaware that my efforts to protect the boundaries of my body had been in vain. I'll never know, and it is a liberating sensation to realize that it doesn't matter if I never know, that the uncertainties of the virus no longer matter. Once the vaccine was in me, the ambiguity and what-ifs and indeterminacy of the past year receded. I'm not sick now, I'm not going to get sick in the future, and I'm not going to make other people sick. That's what I know now. It is both enough and wonderful.

References

Epigraph

Wiman, C. (2013). Excerpt from *My Bright Abyss: Meditations of a Modern Believer*. Farrar, Straus and Giroux. Reprinted by permission of Farrar, Straus and Giroux. All rights reserved.

Introduction

Ngai, S. (2005). *Ugly Feelings*. Harvard University Press.

Breathe

"mouthed my liberal values...": Oglesby, C. (1965, November 27). "Let Us Shape The Future." March on Washington. https://www.sds-1960s.org/sds_wuo/sds_documents/oglesby_future.html

Curiosity Cabinet

Shakespeare, N. (2000). *Bruce Chatwin*. Random House.

All the Futures

"...In terms of a plan?": Bell, J. & Whedon, J. (Writers), & Bell, J. (Director). (2004, May 19). "Not Fade Away." (Season 5, Episode 22) [TV series episode]. In J. Whedon, D. Greenwalt, T. Minear, J. Bell, D. Fury, F. Kuzui, & K. Kuzui (Executive Producers), *Angel*. Mutant Enemy Productions.

Bewildered

Kimmerer, R.W. (2015). *Braiding Sweetgrass: Indigenous Wisdom, Scientific Knowledge, and the Teachings of Plants*. Milkweed Books.
Rogers, R.D. (2015). *Medicinal Plants of Edmonton's River Valley*. CreateSpace Independent Publishing.

Crime and Punishment/Everything is Free

"Entire settlements, entire cities…": Denby, D. (2020, June 22). "The Lockdown
　　　Lessons of 'Crime and Punishment.'" *New Yorker*. https://www.newyorker.com/
　　　magazine/2020/06/29/the-lockdown-lessons-of-crime-and-punishment
Dostoyevsky, F. (1866 [2017]). *Crime and Punishment*. Oxford University Press.
Heyes, C.J. (2020). *Anaesthetics of Existence: Essays on Experience at the Edge*. Duke
　　　University Press.
Welch, G. (2001). "Everything is Free." On *Time (The Revelator)* [CD]. Acony Records.
　　　Lyrics from: https://genius.com/Gillian-welch-everything-is-free-lyrics

The End of Science World

Taylor, C. (2007). *A Secular Age*. Harvard University Press.
Covington, D. (1995). *Salvation on Sand Mountain: Snake Handling and Redemption in
　　　Southern Appalachia*. Da Capo Press.

Why I Can't Think

Reed, L. (1973). "Sweet Jane" [Recorded by The Velvet Underground]. On
　　　Loaded [CD]. Atlantic Records. Lyrics from: https://genius.com/
　　　The-velvet-underground-sweet-jane-lyrics

The River is Alive

Moss, S. (2009). *Names for the Sea: Strangers in Iceland*. Granta.

The Fresh Horrors Device

"…let's see what fresh horrors": Miss O'Kistic (2016, November 10). **wakes up and looks
　　　at phone* ah let's see what fresh horrors await me on the fresh horrors device*
　　　[Tweet]. Twitter. https://twitter.com/missokistic/status/796870708412358657

Pandemic Melancholy

Freud, S. (1917 [1966]). "Mourning and Melancholia." *The Standard Edition of the
　　　Complete Psychological Works of Sigmund Freud, Volume XIV (1914–1916)*
　　　Hogarth Press.
"Code Rocky": Saint Michael's Medical Center (2020, April 16). Youtube. https://www.
　　　youtube.com/watch?v=l1bDT9mk4Vg

Vacation Scandal

Fancourt, D. (2021, January 2). "People Started Breaking Covid Rules When They Saw Those with Privilege Ignore Them." *The Guardian*. https://www.theguardian.com/commentisfree/2021/jan/02/follow-covid-restrictions-break-rules-compliance
Solnit, R. (2010). *A Paradise Built in Hell: The Extraordinary Communities That Arise in Disaster*. Penguin.

Hermits

Finkel, M. (2018). *The Stranger in the Woods: The Extraordinary Story of the Last True Hermit*. Vintage.
Krakauer, J. (1997). *Into the Wild*. Random House.
McCandless, C. (2014). *The Wild Truth*. Harper Collins.
Gonzales, L. (2017). *Deep Survival: Who Lives, Who Dies, and Why*. W.W. Norton.
Fine, J. (2005). *Savage Summit: The True Stories of the First Five Women Who Climbed K2, the World's Most Feared Mountain*. Harper Collins.
Wheeler, S. (2014). *Terra Incognita: Travels in Antarctica*. Modern Library.

Buffalo Bill's Defunct

cummings, e.e. (1920 [1994]). [buffalo bill's]. In R.S. Kennedy (ed.), *E.E. Cummings: Selected Poems*, Liveright.

Ice is Solid and Liquid

Martin, S. (1999, October 21). "Is Glass Really a Liquid?" *Scientific American*. https://www.scientificamerican.com/article/is-glass-really-a-liquid/

No Time at the North Pole

Weeman, K. (2020, March 13). "Time Has No Meaning at the North Pole." *Scientific American*. https://blogs.scientificamerican.com/observations/time-has-no-meaning-at-the-north-pole

Hard Freeze

Robertson, R. (1970). "The Shape I'm In" [Recorded by The Band]. On *Stage Fright* [CD]. Capitol Records. Lyrics from https://www.lyrics.com/lyric/34531815/The+Band/The+Shape+I%27m+In

Falls the Shadow

"Between the conception...": Eliot, T.S. (1922 [2000]). "The Hollow Men." In M.H.
          Abrams and S. Greenblatt (eds.) *Norton Anthology of English Literature 7th ed.*
          Vol 2. W.W. Norton.

Brain Studies

Manseau, P. (2021, February 19). "His Pastors Tried to Steer Him Away from
          Social Media Rage. He Stormed the Capitol Anyway." *Washington*
          Post. https://www.washingtonpost.com/religion/2021/02/19/
          michael-sparks-capitol-siege-jan-6-christian/
"Your brain on grievance...": Kimmel, J. (2020, December 12). "What the Science of
          Addiction Tells Us about Trump." *Politico.* https://www.politico.com/news/
          magazine/2020/12/12/trump-grievance-addiction-444570

This is Your Brain on Covid

Norris, K. (2003). *Acedia and Me: Marriage, Monks and a Writer's Life.* Riverhead.
"...the emotion we're all feeling": Zecher, J. (2020, August 26). "Acedia, the Lost Name
          for the Emotion We're All Feeling Right Now." *The Conversation.*
          https://theconversation.com/acedia-the-lost-name-for-the-emotion-
          were-all-feeling-right-now-144058
Ricard, M., André, C., and Jollien, A. (2020) *Freedom for All of Us: A Monk, A Philosopher,*
          And A Psychiatrist On Finding Inner Peace. Sounds True.

Leonard Cohen at the Whistle Stop Café

Cohen, L. (1974). "There is a War." On *New Skin For the Old Ceremony* [CD]. Columbia.
          Lyrics from: https://genius.com/Leonard-cohen-there-is-a-war-lyrics
Cohen, L. (1992). "The Future." On *The Future* [CD]. Columbia. Lyrics from: https://genius.
          com/Leonard-cohen-the-future-lyrics
Lamott, A. (2021). *Dusk Night Dawn: On Revival and Courage.* Random House.
Cohen, L. (1992). "Anthem." On *The Future* [CD]. Columbia. Lyrics from: https://genius.
          com/Leonard-cohen-anthem-lyrics

Desolation

"...one of the last wilderness areas": UNESCO (2019). "French Austral Lands and Seas".
          UNESCO World Heritage Convention. https://whc.unesco.org/en/list/1603/

"At first, the researchers...": Oskin, B. (2014, February 5). "Greenland's First Coral Reef Found." *Live Science.* https://www.livescience.com/43116-greenland-coral-reef-discovered.html

Other Titles from University of Alberta Press

Next Time There's a Pandemic
VIVEK SHRAYA
"Had I done the lockdown wrong?" Artist Vivek Shraya reflects on how she might have approached pandemic times differently.
CLC KREISEL LECTURE SERIES

Blue Portugal and Other Essays
THERESA KISHKAN
Braided essays about the natural world, aging bodies, family histories, and art and visual phenomena.
WAYFARER SERIES

Little Yellow House
Finding Community in a Changing Neighbourhood
CARISSA HALTON
After moving her family to a neighbourhood with a tough reputation, Halton meets a cast of diverse characters and considers the social and economic forces that shape our cities.

More information at uap.ualberta.ca